# These
# Thousand
# Acres

## Table of Contents

# Prologue

# Gray Mists and Rolling Green Hills

*One's feelings are always in advance of words, so much is deeply felt that is in its very nature indefinable...*
— John Muir (1838-1914)

Although John Muir, a founder of the Sierra Club and adviser to presidents, considered writing to be a poor instrument for conveying the delight, wonder, and enchantment that he experienced in nature, and although he disliked the writing process itself, agonizing over every word, sentence, and paragraph that he wrote, he still managed to produce six volumes of writing during his lifetime. Four additional books were published posthumously. These books, having now been read by millions of people around the world, remain in print to this day. I am one of those millions of Muir readers. John Muir has long been a hero and an inspiration to me. It is my hope, therefore, that in the words that follow I may also express, be it only to some small degree, a portion of the deeply felt delight, wonder, and enchantment that I have experienced while exploring the fields,

View of Malabar Farm from atop Mt. Jeez.

the forests, and the human and natural history of the thousand acres that make up the rolling hills and valleys of a place called Malabar Farm.

It is a curious matter that I can't remember the first time I visited Malabar Farm. Malabar, now a State Park, is located in the rolling countryside of Pleasant Valley, in southern Richland County, Ohio. The farm was once the home of Pulitzer Prize winning author Louis Bromfield. I know that I visited Malabar Farm sometime in the late 1980's, because I have photographs of my daughter Laura that were taken there when she was seven or eight years old, and she was born in 1980. Unfortunately I can't remember that visit, or even what inspired it. It seems that my first experience of Malabar Farm is bound to remain hidden memory, stored somewhere in the recesses of my mind, destined, like so many of my memories, to remain accessible only as a feeling.

Some of the fondest memories of my youth are of summer days spent on my grandfather's small farm in northwestern Pennsylvania. I am able to call forth fragmented pictures in my mind's eye from those days. I suspect, however, that many of these patchwork mental images are in reality only carefully assembled montages, impressions generated from old photographs and oft-told family stories. I trust much more profoundly my wealth of felt memories, memories permeated by intangibles like the scent of newly cut hay on a hot June afternoon, and of the icy cold tartness of plump strawberries plucked from the stem at dawn. Memories of the pungent odor of manure in a dark and aged barn, and of the rough and broken texture of the barn's weathered gray/brown siding. Memories of the pebbly softness of pushing my arms up to my elbows in a bin filled with oats. Memories of the perfect blackness of a star flecked night sky untouched by the glare of street lights or neon signs. It is sensory experiences such as these, only poorly illuminated by the shadow impressions generated in my mind's eye, that ultimately constitute the treasury of my most cherished memories. Having memories that are for the most part built upon a foundation of feelings rather than visual recall has often made communication a struggle. Simply trying to describe my process of drawing out these felt memories has challenged my language skills. It seems that John Muir was right, one's deepest feelings truly are "indefinable". In any event, definable or not, there seems little doubt that these memories are at the root of my interest in and growing appreciation of Malabar Farm.

Fortunately my wife Carolyn is much better at remembering the details of long past events. She can recall the minutest details and remembers well that first trip to Malabar Farm. She especially recalls a specific experience we had there. This was when our young daughter ran ahead of us and across the sloping front lawn of Malabar's "Big House", where she flung her tiny arms around a huge boxer that was sitting statue-like before a screened-in porch. The dog, even while sitting, was nearly as big as she was. My wife momentarily froze in horror, before realizing that the dog was quite child friendly, willingly tolerating Laura's overly enthusiastic attention. We learned later that boxers are especially good dogs if you have young children and want a large dog that will be very protective of them. They are good dogs, that is, if you can tolerate their drooling and slobbering, which can be considerable. In the years that followed I learned that Louis Bromfield loved boxers and that they were a constant presence at Malabar Farm. I now have a copy of a photograph of him standing in a field at Malabar, gathered around him, all vying for his attention, are seven boxers. Wonderful stories of him and his dogs abound. In *Animals and Other People,* a collection of non-fiction short stories published in 1955, Bromfield himself recorded some of his favorite dog centered memories.

It would be ten or twelve years before I would return to Malabar. Throughout the intervening years I thought very little of the farm. I didn't even know that the original main barn, a lofty white edifice built in 1890, had burned down in 1993, ostensibly a victim of a short in an incubator. Fortunately for all of us who have come to love Malabar Farm, the barn was rebuilt in 1994 by the Timber Framers Guild of North America. At 16,000 sq. ft. it was said to have been the largest public barn raising in the United States in more than a hundred years. Looking almost exactly like the original structure, the barn now hosts not only monthly barn dances, a tradition started by Louis Bromfield in the 1940s, but also weddings, receptions, craft shows, and plays. The lower portion of the barn shelters farm animals; cows, sheep, goats, ponies, a rabbit or two, and assorted semi-feral cats. These animal's various vocalizations, especially those of the cattle, have been known to result in some amusing moments during weddings. In the winter, farm equipment is stored in the barn's cavernous interior. Malabar Farm's charm would be much diminished were it not for the efforts of the Timber Framers and their restoration of this iconic Malabar structure.

When I did finally return to Malabar Farm it was in the late 1990s. I was working as an art teacher and I was chaperoning a group of sixth grade students who were visiting the Park as part of a two-day field trip. I participated in these excursions over the next several years and through them became re-acquainted with Malabar Farm and the man who founded it. The summer that I retired after twenty-five years in education I decided to inquire about the possibility of volunteering at Malabar. My knowledge of the Park was still somewhat nascent, and as with the motivation for my first visit there years earlier I can't remember what specific motives drove this action. I didn't recognize it at the time but the phone call that I made to the Park to inquire about volunteering would become one of those pivotal moments that significantly changes the course of one's life. How often these brief occasions pass without particular note. It is only with hindsight that their importance becomes obvious.

I began my time as a volunteer by helping with the many

school groups that visit Malabar on field trips at the end of each school year. Most of these groups are kindergarten through the sixth grade. My primary responsibilities as a volunteer involved introducing the students, most of whom were from the suburbs or the city, to the animals and activities typical of a farm. It was somewhat surprising to learn how few of these children had ever seen a cow close up, "a real cow" as one little girl said. I also frequently led short nature hikes through the woods and fields located near the Park's Visitor Center. In general, I made myself available for just about anything needed of a volunteer, including the many special activities sponsored by the Park; the annual Maple Syrup Festival in March, Ohio Heritage Days in September, and Christmas at Malabar in December.

On a snowy Saturday in mid-February, early in my second year of volunteering, I sat down with Sybil Burskey, Malabar's administrative assistant and coordinator of volunteers, to talk about some programing ideas that were running through my head (In hindsight this may have been a little presumptuous of me.) When we had finished she asked me a simple question. Would I be interested in working at Malabar? As simple as it was, this question caught me completely by surprise. I had not been looking for a job, however by now I had become quite captivated by Malabar Farm and its rich history. This was a history that was no longer limited to the story of Louis Bromfield's return to Pleasant Valley in 1939 and his inspiring work as a writer/farmer dedicated to soil restoration and the wide variety of innovative farming practices that he championed as the "New Agriculture." It was a history that now included many colorful human interest stories that predated Bromfield's arrival, stories that included Indian wars, dark murders, and even bizarre medical practices. Beyond this human history my enthusiasm for Malabar had expanded to include the hiking trails that took me along quiet streams and into hidden forest glens. It extended to the Herefords, Angus, and Shorthorns, and to the sheep and goats that grazed contentedly on Malabar's broad pastures. I even welcomed the pungent odors of the barn and barnyard. I had discovered in all of these things a treasure trove for the senses that transported me back across the decades to those enchanted summer days spent on my grandfather's Pennsylvania farm, back to some of the fondest and most formative memories of my youth. It took me about as long as it takes to draw a breath to tell Sybil that yes, I would be very pleased to work at Malabar, to become a part of its rich heritage.

As a result I became what they call a naturalist-aide at Malabar Farm State Park, my primary responsibilities being that of historic interpretation. I led guided tours of Louis Bromfield's thirty-two room Big House, hosted wagon tours of Malabar's working farm, helped in the gift shop when needed, and in general welcomed visitors to the Park. I continued leading an occasional nature hike in the Park and added a "Malabar History Hike" to the Park's schedule of seasonal activities. I began offering programs about Louis Bromfield and Malabar Farm to interested organizations in the greater regional area, and I created

Louis Bromfield's "Big House", Malabar Farm, Ohio.

one of my favorite programs "A Book Lover's Guide To Louis Bromfield." As I said above, the core of my responsibilities at Malabar involved historic interpretation rather than the traditional naturalist's duties of other Ohio State Parks. The patches on my hat and my shirt did read "naturalist," however, and on occasion this caused problems, as for example when a Park visitor would ask me to identify some unfamiliar plant, butterfly, or pond turtle. I continued my Malabar work for five wonderful years before retiring for a second time and returning to my volunteering activities. At that time I also expanded my involvement beyond volunteering by joining the Malabar Farm Foundation, where I continue to work for the preservation of this jewel of the Ohio State Parks.

Mornings are my favorite time at Malabar, that time when the farm is quiet and the animals still, that time of soft mists floating over pale green fields of dew dampened timothy grass and red clover, that time when the eastern sky is streaked with faint ribbons of pink and purple, the sun still only a promise on the horizon. It was on just such a bucolic summer morning that I first gave voice to my impressions of Malabar with the words "these thousand acres."[1] The words came to me as I turned into the lane that leads to the Park's Visitor Center. Louis Bromfield's Big House and his great white barn, their hard lines softened by the wispy vale of a thinning fog, rose dramatically to my left, a pleasing background to the undulations of a gently rolling pasture dotted with grazing cattle. Those three words, "these thousand acres," quickly assumed a quality that was infused with meaning, a meaning that seemed to arise spontaneously, new and complete, though in some primal way I am sure that it had to have been percolating in my subconscious for quite some time. It was only on that morning, however, that I became overtly cognizant of just how deeply those thousand acres of Malabar Farm had impacted my life. Malabar Farm had provided opportunities for me that were the things of dreams. At the risk of sounding overly dramatic, I consider it to have been my great good fortune and my unique privilege to have worked at Malabar Farm State Park, to have wandered freely through rooms once lived in by a unique individual named Louis Bromfield, to have become a part, if only in some small way, of the on-going story of Malabar Farm. I continue to find pleasure in ambles down the dirt lane that weaves its way through the fields Louis Bromfield so lovingly restored. I look forward with enthusiasm to hikes through the woodlands to which he gave new life. I hope to continue these journeys, and the musings they inspire, long into the future.

In the days and months that followed my early morning epiphany, that simple phrase "these thousand acres" continued to roll around in my head. Exactly what feelings had I brought forth and given verbal expression to with those three words? How could I define exactly what it was that had drawn them out? What was I trying to say, what deeper contemplations might be seeking the light of day? What precisely was it about Malabar Farm that inspired such thinking? Slowly the answers to these questions began to come together. Many things about that unique land, things beyond even those cherished memories of my youth, blend seamlessly with my present interests: **Reading**: Louis Bromfield was a Pulitzer Prize winning author of thirty-two books and I had already read several of them. **History**: An amazing number of the down-to-earth "common man" stories of the America frontier are found in this land that had inspired Bromfield. **Hiking**: the acreage of Malabar Farm offers some twelve miles of trails, many of them through the heavily wooded hillsides that were so loved by Bromfield. **Art and Photography**: Malabar Farm is a visual artist's delight. As all of these things came together in my mind a new thought slowly emerged. Perhaps there might be material here for a book, a book that would tell the story of this countryside that Louis Bromfield had stitched together to create his beloved Malabar Farm, a farm that through his tireless teaching and lecturing, and through his voluminous agricultural writing (five books and more than 100 magazine and journal articles), he would within a decade make into "the most famous farm in America."

By way of a vaguely ethereal process the phrase "these thousand acres" had come to me out of the gray mists and the rolling green hills of Malabar. Thoughts of this book, *These Thousand Acres: The Story of the Land That Became Malabar Farm,* developed only bit by bit out of my reflections on those three words. It wasn't at all clear to me how to proceed with such a project. The raw material was there, I knew that for certain, but I had to figure out how to organize it, how to build a structure on which to could hang the story of Malabar. This was a new experience for me. I had written many papers in college, some of them quite good if I do say so myself, but writing a book was a different matter. At first I thought in terms of a relatively straight forward history, but the more I struggled with that idea, the more awkward the process became. The tale of the land that became Malabar Farm was more than a recitation of facts or a chronological recording of this and that event. At one point I nearly gave up on the project. It just wasn't working out the way I wanted. I was frustrated, sensing that I wasn't getting at the essence of what makes Malabar Farm the special place that it is.

It was about this time, in one of those fortuitous moments, that I discovered a book by John Elder titled *Reading the Mountains of Home,* a book I had nearly passed up while browsing the shelves of a used book store. In this book Elder, a professor of English and Environmental Studies at Middlebury College, describes a series of hikes that he made through the re-forested wilds of North and South Mountains near his home in Bristol, Vermont. Elder coupled descriptions of his walks with passages from Robert Frost's wonderful poem "Directive." By using this poem as something akin to a field guide Elder was able to add illumination, depth, and richness to his descriptions of the natural world that he encountered on his hikes, to the eroding human artifacts he observed, and to the slowly vanishing traces of past habitation that he discovered. *Reading the Mountains of*

*Home* isn't a history book, or even a nature book. Rather it is one man's personal account of life passages, an account that dares to address the inevitable and unavoidable natural and universal changes that must be experienced by each of us as we travel life's often crooked path. This volume has become one of my favorite books. I have re-read it several times and gain something new from it with each new reading.

Perhaps here, within the pages of Elder's *Reading The Mountains of Home,* was the suggestion of a structure I might borrow for my own writing. I could reveal the story of Malabar Farm within the context of a series of hikes, walks that would not only take the reader through the wanderings of my own mind and its reflections on the history imbedded in the land that became Malabar Farm, but would also reveal the best of the natural world that Malabar has to offer today. Moreover these walks would lend themselves to the telling of the long and rich story of "these thousand acres," a story that was already ages old long before there was a Malabar Farm, or even a Louis Bromfield for that matter. I eventually settled on five hikes situated within the borders of the Park. However, in planning these hikes I quickly discovered that I couldn't write about Malabar Farm in isolation.

Many of the captivating events and activities that made this area what it is had their origins beyond the official boundaries of the Park itself. These events and activities flowed into Malabar's acres from a much wider world. The land that became Malabar Farm wasn't an island, it never had been, and I couldn't write about it as though it were. To tell the story properly two of my five hikes would have to pass beyond the legal boundaries of the Park. I also concluded that the book needed an opening chapter dedicated to the story of the founder of Malabar Farm. Malabar Farm was Louis Bromfield's dream. Without him there would be no Park today. Few people would give a second thought to the rich history of the place Bromfield loved and made famous, the place he called home.

Where such local histories do manage to survive, they are most often buried within the yellowing pages of ancient, dust covered tomes, books stacked on the little visited shelves of county historical societies. It is because of this that Louis Bromfield's creation of Malabar Farm, and especially his writing that celebrated the farm, is important. Enfolded within the history of Malabar's thousand acre world exists in miniature a snow-globe world that by its very nature contains components that are universal. Within this landscape the reader will find a narrative that passes beyond the merely local, beyond the experiences of individual personalities, a narrative that not only embraces the foibles of human societies and the peculiarities of entire civilizations and cultures, but also reaches back to ages so far removed from today's experience as to seem almost incomprehensible.

In the words that follow I offer my testimony to a personal love affair with Malabar Farm. Here is the engaging story of the land that for a while stood as America's most famous farm. Any mistakes are unintentional and mine alone. My hope is that in the pages that follow you will also come to embrace something of the wonder and joy I have found here, that your life will be enriched through the reading of these pages, and that you will be inspired to experience the hills, valleys and woodlands of Malabar Farm for yourself. Perhaps we will meet on some future Malabar visit. I look forward to that time.

Tom Bachelder
Shiloh, Ohio

# Chapter 1

# Coming Home

*...Louis Bromfield, a force of nature acting*
*in his own epic agrarian drama.*
— Richard Gilbert
*Shepherd: A Memoir* (2014)

It was a cold Ohio day in December of 1938, the countryside buried deep in snow. A heavy gray sky hung low overhead, the short winter afternoon rapidly drawing to a close. Long blue shadows of the approaching evening stretched icy fingers across silent fields. Golden points of light began to twinkle at the windows of lonely farmsteads. Pleasant Valley in southern Richland County was once again settling into the hibernation of a long, dark, and still winter's night.

At first the car appeared little more than a tiny black beetle crawling slowly through the darkening distance. It would appear for a moment on the crest of a hill, only to vanish as it followed the roller coaster ups and downs of the Pin Hook Road. Gradually as it came closer the beetle transformed itself into an automobile. Moving in halts and starts the driver, seemingly unsure of himself, would crane his head out the window, the cold wind ruffling his unruly hair. Looking up and down the road and across deep vistas, his eyes would settle momentarily on the warm glow of windows in distant farmhouses and then move on. He appeared to be searching for something, something perhaps only half remembered. The driver of that vehicle wasn't just anyone; he was world famous author Louis Bromfield, and on that cold December day he had come home, home to the memories of a childhood spent exploring this same rural landscape.

December of 1938 found Louis Bromfield, his wife Mary, and Bromfield's friend and longtime business manager George Hawkins, driving through the snow covered landscape of rural southern Richland County, Ohio. Much had changed in the decades since he had been away and Bromfield was finding it difficult to locate recognizable landmarks. After many hours of scouring the countryside he turned onto Pleasant Valley Road. The valley opened up before him and in a flash of recognition Louis knew he had found what he was looking for.

In the darkening shadows, Bromfield was able to pick out familiar landmarks from decades earlier. To his right stood an ancient and dignified two story red brick house. Now, however, it seemed to shrink back from him, embarrassed to be seen in a coat of pallid yellow some fool had painted over it. This house, the old Schrack Place, had an honorable history. It deserved better. Nestled in a copse of trees on the hillside behind the house rested a gray and weather-worn spring house. Through the hand-hewn stone troughs of that aging building flowed a delightful stream, its clear and icy-cold water emerging from massive sandstone cliffs nearby. The ice encrusted stream disappeared into a culvert beneath the road as Bromfield's car passed. A short distance beyond the house, looming impressively before a brooding charcoal sky, was the hill. It now carried the derisive name of Poverty Knob and had done so for at least a generation. It was said that if you climbed to its rounded top you would find yourself standing on the roof of the county. To Bromfield's far left, beyond the barren December fields that defined the bottom lands of Pleasant Valley, flowed Switzer Creek, its course now etched roughly against an imposing wooded hillside by a skeletal white line of sycamore trees. Memories of unmeasured time spent with his father exploring that very creek's rock strewn banks, fishing in its many deep pools, and exploring the high sandstone ledges that framed it, welled up in the author's mind.

Tracking the flow of Switzer Creek upstream, Bromfield's

eyes came to rest on a distant farmstead sheltered beneath a steep, rock faced embankment. In the closing darkness the fading outline of the farmhouse remained identifiable by the warm and welcoming lantern glow that emanated from its numerous curtained windows. Near the house stood a massive red barn, a barn that harkened back to the time when this valley, along with many others similar to it throughout the county, was proudly recognized as a "rich land".

The Clement Herring farmstead, c.1938   photograph courtesy Malabar Farm State Park

In a fit of spontaneity characteristic of his nature, Louis Bromfield, in rapid succession turned his car left onto Hastings Road, crossed the narrow and creaking bridge over Switzer Creek, rounded a sharp bend to the right, followed the road over a low rise, discovered a driveway on his right, and started the climb up a sloping and snow covered lane that led him to the front of the farmhouse with the great red barn. Any other plans that he may have been deliberating upon were quickly put aside. This place was calling to him. He had heard that call before, if only as a faint echo across decades and oceans. As he neared the old farmhouse the whisper that had impelled him to write *The Farm* and *The Man Who Had Everything* became clarion, an undeniable shout.

15

Approaching the front door Louis knocked tentatively and then more vigorously. After a few moments it opened slowly and an elderly white haired woman clothed in a flour dusted gingham apron peered out. Louis introduced himself, then gestured toward the woman waiting in the car behind him,"That's my wife Mary, behind her is my good friend George." Introductions having been completed to his satisfaction, and with an abruptness characteristic of his nature, he asked the lady with the gingham apron if she would be interested in selling her farm, assuring her that he would give her a fair price. Momentarily taken aback by the brusqueness of the stranger's sudden appearance and laconic question she, nevertheless, recovered quickly and, perhaps a bit to his surprise, said that there might be something to discuss, but that he would have to speak with her husband. He could find him in the barn. With an amiable smile she then completed the formalities that had been short-circuited by Bromfield's earlier exuberance, "My name is Maude Herring, my husband is Clement." Apologizing for his earlier curtness Louis then walked toward the barn. Mrs. Herring gestured for Mary and George to join her inside.

Mr. Herring's head was crowned with a thick crop of graying hair. Dressed in frayed blue denim overalls and a woolen overcoat, he moved slowly with a slightly stooped back, evidence of a lifetime of hard work. Louis found him in the milking parlor cleaning a piece of equipment that he had just finished repairing. Following an introduction more appropriate to the occasion, Louis explained his reason for bothering Mr. Herring at that late hour. With the old farmer's barn work and evening chores now complete, Louis was invited to join him in Maude's kitchen. This was a matter that he and Mrs. Herring would have to consider together. With that, the world famous author and the elderly, gray-haired farmer entered the old house with the warm and welcoming lantern glow in its windows.

A congress of serendipitous events came together that winter evening over oatmeal cookies and coffee. The Herrings were, in fact, interested in selling their farm, all 247 acres of it, along with their house, the great barn that sat near it, and all of the stock and equipment. Clem Herring was a good farmer. He loved his farm, every square foot of it; the soil now buried deep beneath banks of snow, the fat cattle resting secure in his great barn, even the little creek with its icy waters that carried the chill of winter through the lower pasture. He had labored all of his life to ensure the continuing productivity of his land. Clem and Maude had children, but they had gone to the city, and none had any interest in being farmers. Clem was now nearing 80 and the farm work was becoming more challenging with each passing season. Briers and small trees encroached on formerly pristine fields and pastures. Fences and out buildings were in need of repairs that he could no longer keep up with. Convinced of Louis Bromfield's sincere desire to nurture the land as they had, a deal was struck that December evening as the Herrings and Bromfield's gathered around a warm stove and a plate of cookies. The Bromfield's would became the newest farm family in Pleasant Valley.

In the darkening shadows of that cold winter's eve a seventeen year adventure would begin, an adventure that would see Louis Bromfield's literary reputation suffer, but an adventure that in the decade to come would also see Malabar Farm become the most famous farm in America. On that December night in 1938 Louis Bromfield was to begin a journey that would end with him being called "The Father of Sustainable Agriculture."

Louis Bromfield had always admired Thomas Jefferson and he embraced Jefferson's economic and social philosophy of the yeoman farmer. Men who owned and worked their own farms were the backbone of a nation. Secure on their farms, these men would guarantee the strength and independence of the country. By 1938, as he looked at the current state of agriculture, politics, and the economy, Bromfield had become something of a pessimist.

Though he had lived in Europe during the years of the American Dust Bowl, he had made several trips to the States and was well aware of the vast environmental and economic devastation carried in the Dust Bowl's wake. He knew of the droughts that fostered blinding dust storms, storms that stripped the land of its top soil, storms that sucked the life out of crops. He knew of the human lives broken and the families destroyed by the abject poverty that inevitably followed.

At the beginning of his Malabar adventure, Bromfield did not in tend to participate in an agricultural revolution. He simply wanted to fulfill the dream of farm ownership that he had nurtured for so long. Bromfield believed that agriculture was the foundation for all other human economic activity, and agriculture was in trouble. It wasn't only in the states that had been directly impacted by the Dust Bowl. All across the entire nation, soils were being mined rather than farmed, the land depleted of valuable nutrients in the name of short term gains. Underground water resources were being exhausted by ill-informed irrigation plans. Fields and pasture lands were eroding into the nation's streams and rivers, ultimately to be lost in the expanding deltas at river's end. The demands of a growing human population, weakened though it was by poor nutrition, only exacerbated the problem. All of this had a profound impact on the thinking of the boy from Mansfield, Ohio, the boy who had grown up to become a world famous author, the author who had now come home. Louis Bromfield wanted to create a farm that would produce the full range of foods required for a healthy diet. It was to be a self-sufficient island of security, a sanctuary for family and friends during difficult times.

A month after acquiring the Herring Place in January of 1939 Bromfield added the Beck Farm to what would become Malabar Farm. This property adjoined the Herring Farm on the east and added over a hundred more acres to Malabar Farm. Both of these purchases were made in the depths of the winter with fields buried beneath five or six inches of snow. In the spring, when he had opportunity to actually walk the land that had become his, Louis quickly learned that although the Herring place was in fairly good condition, a significant portion of Beck's acres consisted of badly eroded land and exhausted soil, some of it so poor that the only thing it seemed capable of supporting in abundance was weeds. With this discovery Bromfield concluded that he needed to take his farm in a new direction, a direction that would change his life, a direction that would also contribute significantly to the transformation of agriculture in America.

Malabar Farm would become an experimental farm, a farm where Bromfield would find solutions to the most glaring agricultural problems of the day, problems that had been building for years, problems that he believed were reaching a critical mass. Malabar Farm would be a showplace for farming practices that Louis Bromfield would soon call "The New Agriculture." To this end Bromfield hired as his first farm manager a young man named Max Drake. In this endeavor Bromfield and Drake were not working in isolation. Bromfield had come to Pleasant Valley on the tail end of the Dust Bowl years, years that had seen half of the top soil in America's Midwest blow away, the result of severe drought and poor farming practices. Both men, but especially Bromfield, became involved with a number of government and non-government agencies and organizations that were working to help farmers restore and preserve their land.

It was Drake who actually initiated many of the earliest changes that would define the direction and the look of Malabar Farm. With Drake placed in charge Bromfield left for Hollywood where he was to serve as consultant for the 20th Century Fox film *The Rains Came,* a major motion picture set in India, based on his best-selling 1937 novel of the same title. This film would go on to win an Academy Award for Special Effects in 1939. The income from this novel and the subsequent film gave Bromfield much of the money he needed to begin his farming career at Malabar.

When Bromfield left for California he did so with images in his mind of a farm laid out in the traditional rectangular and checker-board fields of his youth. Max Drake, trained in new techniques and creative in his approach to farming, soon realized that there was a better way to organize his fields. Erosion was a serious problem on the farm. Deep gullies scored the land and were slowly leaching what remained of Malabar's valuable top soil into Switzer Creek. Drake recognized that it was the old way of plowing straight up and down hilly fields, plowing that was defined by the straight lines of conventional square and rectangle fields that was the root of the problem. Something new was required. Drake began laying out fields in lines that followed the contours of Malabar's hills and valleys. Plowing would now climb hills by circling around them rather than running straight up and over the top. These contour furrows would become narrow terraces moving perpendicular to the lines of incline. They would catch and hold rainwater, giving it time to soak in. Water and soil would no longer race downhill through ever deepening gullies and into the nearest stream-bed.

Working in Hollywood for months Bromfield had no idea of the changes happening back home. When he returned to Malabar Farm for the first time he was outraged by what he saw. His farm bore no semblance of the farm he had expected to see. Drake was nearly fired. Fortunately Louis Bromfield was willing to consider different points of view if intelligently argued and took the time to listen. Once Drake had an opportunity to explain the theory behind his plan, and once Bromfield actually saw it working during heavy rains, he was convinced. Contour plowing, a technique previously known but little used, would become one of the core elements Bromfield would promote to prevent soil erosion.

In 1942 Bromfield would add the old Schrack Place to his farm, at that time in the hands of an absentee owner named

Neiman. Two years earlier Bromfield had also purchased a smaller triangular piece of wooded land further down Switzer Creek that he called the "Jungle". He now owned about 600 acres outright and would soon lease another 200 or so acres from the Muskingum Watershed Conservancy at Pleasant Hill Reservoir, two miles east of Malabar. These purchases and the land leased from Pleasant Hill brought the total land under Malabar management to about 800 acres. With the Schrack Farm came the sad and much abused hill called Poverty Knob. At its foot stood the defaced and forlorn brick house beside the great spring.

Of all his purchases the old Schrack farm was in the worst condition, the land having been badly mistreated for years by ignorant and thoughtless tenant farmers. This time, however, Bromfield knew what he was getting for his money. He knew that the farm had been leased for many years and that the tenants farming it cared little for the soil, that they took all they could from the land and gave nothing back. Year after year the farm's crop yields had declined, until eventually the absentee owner couldn't find a local farmer interested in leasing his land. Poverty Knob, later renamed Mount Jeez by Bromfield, had gullies running down its sides deep enough to swallow a tractor. The 120 year old pallid yellow brick house was still there to rent out, but in its deteriorating condition even that was quickly losing its appeal to all but the lowest elements of the rural community. This much abused farm would be Bromfield's greatest challenge. If he could restore this place he could do it anywhere. And he would do the work using techniques any farmer could employ. Fifty or five thousand acres, it didn't matter, his "New Agriculture" wouldn't require the purchase of expensive new equipment. It would, however, demand a new way of thinking about how one worked with his land.

The seventy acres that made up "The Jungle" were something different. Here was a triangular piece of land bordering the southern edge of the Schrack property. Switzer Creek flowed through the heart of this ground. The Jungle was luxuriously wild and heavily wooded. This land was completely at odds with the impoverished fields nearby. Many of the Jungle's acres were low and lush in both flora and fauna, supporting a small fen bordered by willows, and filled with cattails. In the dark brown mud of early spring skunk cabbage pushed mottled, horn-like spikes skyward through late snow that they melted with 70 degrees of self-generated heat. In summer the drying rushes and sedges waved gently in warm breezes that blew down the valley. Red-wing blackbirds found refuge in dense undergrowth or perched stately on the heads of cattails. Whitetail deer found year-round sanctuary in scattered thickets. From early May through mid-September, wildflowers blanketed the floor of the Jungle with an exuberant rainbow of hues, yellow trout lily, white dutchmen's-breeches, orange jewel weed, blue phlox, marsh marigold, and wild violets in purple, white and yellow. All these flowers and dozens more dressed the woodlands in a confetti explosion of unrestrained color.

Switzer Creek and the marshy bottom lands of the Jungle were bordered to the north and south by dry hillsides blanketed with assorted hardwoods, maturing trees that formed a distinct boundary separating the Jungle from the fields of the old Schrack Place and the high ridge topped by Ferguson Meadow. In the summer the damp riparian environment along Switzer Creek was carpeted with soft mosses and the broad leaves of countless skunk cabbages. The pale greens of lichen mixed with the brilliant oranges of fungus to paint both rocks and fallen trees. The exposed muddy edges of the stream temporarily preserved the tracks of wandering deer, raccoon, mink, and countless other tiny forest creatures. The Jungle, a mere seventy acres, was the most biologically diverse environment to be found at Malabar Farm. Louis Bromfield loved it. No plow would ever touch this varied ground, no chainsaw would disturb its earthy tranquility.

Early in the 1940s a gentleman named Ed Faulkner came to see Louis Bromfield. Faulkner, the author of *Plowman's Folly,* was a passionate advocate of a farming practice he called no-till plowing and he had come to Malabar Farm to recruit Bromfield to his cause. No-till plowing did away with the traditional moldboard plow, the plow that in one form or another had been used on American farms since colonial times. This was the iconic plow that had broken the virgin soils of countless pioneer farms across the continent and it held a time honored place in the barns and in the hearts of many a weather-worn and leathery-faced farmer. However, according to Faulkner, moldboard plowing was a problem for two very important reasons. By design this plow dug deeply into the ground, turning over great mounds of earth and exposing the bared soil to serious erosion from both wind and rain. Moldboard plowing also tended to bury any surface organic debris under heaps of dirt, where it would often ferment before it could decompose naturally and thus enrich the soil. Faulkner advocated planting each new season's crop within the organic debris left on the surface from the previous year. This organic debris, what Louis Bromfield called green manure, would provide a ground cover that would minimize soil erosion, reduce moisture evaporation, and, being left on or near the surface, decompose in a more natural way.

Bromfield was at first skeptical. Hadn't moldboard plows proven their worth over many generations of use? However, as he had done earlier with Max Drake, he listened to Faulkner's impassioned reasoning and slowly began to see the possibilities in Faulkner's carefully crafted arguments. When he tried the technique for himself, and witnessed the results, he became a convert. Louis Bromfield became an early practitioner of a process that would eventually become standard on many farms, not only in America, but also around the world. He began to promote no-till plowing widely and aggressively, and it soon become an important component in his expanding campaign to restore, improve, and preserve the agricultural soils of America.

By the mid-1940s Malabar Farm had become known well

enough that Bromfield was receiving dozens of letters every day asking questions and seeking advice. Hundreds of visitors were arriving weekly to see for themselves what Bromfield was writing about in countless farm magazines and what he was saying in hundreds of speeches. Knowing that he didn't have enough hours in the day to respond to all those seeking his advice, Louis Bromfield began writing what would eventually become his four volume series of non-fiction farm books. The first of these, *Pleasant Valley* was published in 1945. It quickly became a bestseller. One critic compared it favorably to Henry David Thoreau's *Walden.* This praise came in sharp contrast to the negative reviews then being written about his current fiction, fiction that Bromfield found necessary to continue producing in order to support not only his expensive experimental farm operations, but also the rather rich lifestyle that he enjoyed in his Big House at Malabar. He had lost interest in writing fiction and acknowledged that his current work was not of the quality of his earlier novels. Nonetheless the sharp words of critics still stung.

In 1944 Bromfield published a novel titled *What Became of Anna Bolton.* Edmund Wilson, one of the most influential literary critics of the day, wrote a review of the book and titled it "What Became of Louis Bromfield." This piece was less a review and more a personal diatribe directed at the author himself. Wilson savagely attacked Bromfield and what he saw as the woefully unfulfilled promise of the author's earlier work. In only a few hundred words, Edmund Wilson managed to destroy much of what remained of Louis Bromfield's once bright literary reputation. His novels would continue to sell well to a large and loyal fan base, and he would remain a favorite of his publishers, but most critics now dismissed him as a serious novelist.

While Bromfield's reputation as a novelist was declining his reputation as an innovative farmer with something important to say was growing. Farm groups from across the nation were now inviting him to speak. He traveled widely, giving speeches to state agricultural associations, granges, garden clubs, and FFA groups. He even traveled overseas, lecturing before groups in England, France, New Zealand, and South Africa. At his busiest he was giving over a hundred speeches a year. Add to this the thousands of visitors now being hosted annually at Malabar and it is a wonder that Bromfield had time to write. However, write he did, publishing a total of seventeen books between 1940 and 1955, including fiction, non-fiction, collections of short stories, countless articles for farm journals and magazines, and even a syndicated newspaper column "Voice From the Country." Moreover, he did it all while still actively engaged in the operations of his farm.

In the late spring of 1945 a singular event occurred at Malabar that would bring the farm to the attention of the millions of people across the nation who were not farmers. While working in New York City in the early1920s Louis Bromfield had met a young and aspiring actor named Humphrey Bogart. A friendship developed between the two men that would last for the remainder of their lives. Now, two decades later, Humphrey Bogart was a famous actor and he brought Lauren Bacall to his friend's country home in Ohio to be married. On May 21, 1945, with Louis Bromfield serving as best man, Humphrey Bogart and Lauren Bacall were wed before the twin staircases in the foyer of Malabar's Big House. Newspapers, magazines, radio broadcasts, and movie house newsreels quickly carried word of the marriage to a world enthralled by motion picture stars and all things Hollywood. The Bogie and Bacall wedding at Malabar Farm was the biggest entertainment story of the summer, and Malabar Farm shared in the attention. Its place on the map of American popular culture was now assured.

By 1948 Malabar Farm was being called the most famous farm in America. In that year Bromfield published his second farm book *Malabar Farm.* In it he added to the story of the restoration of his land. Bromfield continued his innovative work at Malabar, and continued telling the world about that work. He even had a Saturday morning NBC radio broadcast from the Big House. In this program he spoke on various topics ranging from politics to the New Agriculture. His subjects included the importance of crop rotation and the study of trace elements in soil. Crop rotation in particular was to become another of those core elements in Louis' soil restoration program. The practice of crop rotation was known and used by some farmers before Bromfield, but it wasn't employed widely until he began promoting its importance as a way to preserve the productivity of cultivated fields. Repeated single-crop-planting was hard on the soil and required the application of significant amounts of expensive fertilizers to keep the land producing acceptable crop yields. In the beginning of his farm operations at Malabar Bromfield acknowledged that on his poorest fields he found it necessary to use a significant amount of fertilizer in order to get healthy crops growing once again, but he also said that in the years that followed he had been able to reduce this dependence of fertilizers by nearly 95 percent.

In April of 1948 Bromfield's business manager, secretary, and good friend George Hawkins died unexpectedly. Hawkins had been with Bromfield since 1929 and he was essential to the financial well being of the farm. It was Hawkins who kept Bromfield writing the novels that supported not only the work of Malabar Farm, but also Bromfield's generous lifestyle as well. Bromfield never liked dealing with the details required in matters of money. He was good at making it, and especially good at spending it, but was a poor manager of the stuff. Hawkins' death marked the beginning of money problems that would mount steadily in coming years. Bromfield also suffered other personal losses that followed closely on the heels of Hawkins' death. In the early 1950s, within two weeks of each other, his daughters Hope and Ellen had married and moved away. In September of 1952 Louis' wife Mary died at the age of sixty. Experiments on the farm were expensive, Hollywood studios had stopped calling, and the bottom had fallen out of agricultural prices.

Without Hawkins to goad him into writing fiction Bromfield would produce only one more novel. *Mr. Smith* was published in 1951, and critics quickly attacked, labeling it his worst work. One critic went so far as to say that it should never have been written. A loyal public, eager for all that he wrote did, however, assure that this final novel sold well. Never tiring of the pen, Bromfield continued to write enthusiastically about his farm, publishing *Out of the Earth* in 1950 and *From My Experience* in 1955. His final book *Animals and Other People*, a collection of previously published non-fiction short stories, was also published in 1955. *From My Experience,* the last volume of his series of farm books, is a particularly moving account. In that book Bromfield wrote not only of the wealth of practical things he had learned in his years of working at Malabar Farm, but also of how his experiences on the land had enriched his life and spirit. To that end he wrote of coming upon the book *Out of My Life and Thought,* by Albert Schweitzer. From that volume Bromfield quoted a brief passage that, short though it was, had had an immediate and profound effect upon him.

*"Reverence for life affords me my fundamental principle of morality,namely that good consists in maintaining, assisting, and enhancing life,and that to destroy, to harm, or to hinder life is evil."*

Bromfield was especially moved by Schweitzer's phrase *"reverence for life."* For him these three simple words succinctly summed up what he had been striving to say and to do for years. They became something of an anthem for Bromfield, encapsulating all that he had devoted his life and energy to at Malabar Farm.

Louis Bromfield    photograph courtesy Malabar Farm State Park.

In *From My Experience* Bromfield also wrote of his plans for the future, a future that he may well have already suspected wasn't likely to happen. In 1954 he had learned that he had bone cancer, an illness that he kept from most family and friends. In spite of this illness Bromfield continued filling his days with activities and plans that progressively taxed what remained of his waning energy. He continued to write about agriculture, to travel for speeches and to work at Malabar. His days remained full. This work was, however, increasingly interrupted by secret treatments that he received for the cancer that was slowly killing him. Louis Bromfield would die less than a year after the publication of *From My Experience.* Knowing this, the passages in which he had written so hopefully of the future make for some quite poignant reading.

Late in February, 1956 Louis Bromfield collapsed at his

home and was taken to University Hospital in Columbus, Ohio. Having kept the graveness of his condition to himself, he was expected to return home soon. Suffering not only from cancer but also from pneumonia, jaundice and hepatitis that he had contracted from treatments for the cancer, Bromfield was far sicker than even his closest friends suspected. For two weeks, illness notwithstanding, he managed to maintain a steady correspondence with friends and associates. In his final week his condition declined rapidly and the letters stopped.

Louis Bromfield died on March 18, 1956 at the age of fifty-nine years and four months. He was buried at Olivet Cemetery, Malabar Farm, surrounded by the fields and pastures he loved.[2] A bright star of both the arts and the earth had burned out too quickly. Malabar remained, however, and in future years would become his most enduring legacy.[3]

Louis Bromfield c.1945, photograph courtesy Malabar Farm State Park

*The adventure at Malabar is by no means finished ...*
*The land came to us out of eternity and when the youngest*
*of us associated with it dies, it will still be here.*

– Louis Bromfield, *Pleasant Valley* 1945

# Chapter 2

# A Walk Among Native Roots

Bordering the northern side of Pleasant Valley Road, about three-quarters of a mile west of Malabar Farm, is a massive and craggy wall of sandstone that defines that part of Pleasant Valley for several hundred yards. The pock-marked face of this natural escarpment is coarsely fragmented by numerous deep crevices. These irregular cracks combine with the sandstone's compressed layers of sedimentation to cut the rock surface into a rough horizontal patchwork of tan, burnt umber, and dirty yellow segments. Ferns, backed by a curtain of tall trees, crown the cliff's fractured upper edges. Near this formation's eastern end, a jagged prominence rises some thirty feet above the valley floor. Here the rock juts forward like the prow of a great ship. Mottled splotches of green moss and pale lichen color the point's shadowy lower surfaces. On the ground at the base of the point rests a jumble of angular and broken boulders. In the summer this towering sandstone edifice is easily missed by motorists, hidden as it is behind the thicket of trees and shrubs that climb to the cliff's stony foot. This sandstone prominence is known as Pipe's Cliff, and there is a story to be told in the name.

Captain Pipe's Cliff.

Unfortunately, an abandoned and badly weathered A-frame structure now rests atop the point. Perhaps this building once served a better purpose, but today it is little more than an eyesore.

The man known to white settlers as Captain Pipe was a chief of the Monsey branch of the Lenape Indians, the tribe known to pioneers, fur traders, and settlers as the Delaware. Although the cliff now bears his name, Captain Pipe was not present on that day in 1781 when, fleeing punishment that awaited them in Pennsylvania for suspected assaults on white settlers, a small group of Lenape paused to rest on the crest of the high sandstone outcropping. With them were Pipe's sister Onalsaka, her husband Round Head, and their new baby. The high point where the cliff formed a wedge that jutted outward into the broad valley below them, gave the Indians a clear view across the landscape. Moving cautiously down this valley under the leadership of a Captain Broadhead was a squad of pursuing soldiers. From their vantage point on the cliff high above, the Indians spotted the soldiers before they themselves were seen.

Apparently panicked by what they saw, several Indians foolishly fired on the soldiers, the white smoke from their muskets revealing their hidden location. Quickly recovering from this surprise attack the soldiers returned fire, shooting blindly in the direction of the white smoke that wafted across the rocky heights above them. Onalsaka, infant in her arms, stood at cliff's edge, momentarily stunned by the unexpected blast of gun fire that had exploded near her. Musket balls from the soldier's rapid return fire ripped through branches near her. Suddenly Onalsaka, still clutching her child, pitched forward, struck in the breast by a ball. She and the baby fell to their deaths, smashing onto the rocks far below. Unsure of their foe's numbers, the soldiers promptly withdrew and Round Head recovered the bodies of his wife and baby. He buried them at the bottom of the cliff where they had fallen. It was said that for many years Captain Pipe annually visited the cliff, where he offered prayers to honor his sister's memory. Eventually this high rocky outcropping came to be known as Pipe's Cliff.

The veracity of the story of Pipe's Cliff has always been questioned, but the presence of the Lenape in southern Richland County before the arrival of the first pioneer settlers has never been in doubt. While significant evidence exists demonstrating that prehistoric Indians occupied this region long ago, the Lenape hadn't arrived much earlier than the white men. Coming from eastern Pennsylvania in the mid 18th century, the Lenape settled on lands in the upper Ohio River basin, having been invited there by their ancient allies the Wyondats. On several occasions in the past I had heard vague references of an old Lenape Indian village called Helltown that had once been located in the southern part of Richland County. A name like Helltown produces evocative images of drunken Indians, bloody brawls, and the general debauchery so often associated with the alcohol besotted and desperate last days of many Native American tribes before they were forever driven out of their homelands and onto reservations. Even Louis Bromfield, writing of the early pioneer history of Richland County in *Pleasant Valley,* referred to the Indians of those days as *"...dirty, drunken animals."*

I first came across the name Helltown recorded in print in a 1908 history of Richland County in the public library. In this book Helltown was identified as a Lenape Indian village that once stood on a bluff on the right bank of the Clearfork River about a mile and a half downstream from the town of Newville. Its location was further pinpointed several hundred yards upstream from where Switzer Creek flowed into the Clearfork. From this county history I also learned that my assumptions concerning the name Helltown and the nature of the community that lived there were decidedly in error.

At the time of first European contacts in the 16th and early

17th centuries the Lenape were living in the eastern coastal area known as the Northeastern Woodlands. In rough terms this region was made up of the land around and between the Delaware and the Hudson Rivers. The Lenape soon became involved in an extensive fur trade with the European settlers. For a time the Lenape had thrived on this trade with white men, but by the early years of the 18th century fur bearing animals were becoming scarce in the Lenape homeland. The European trade goods that the Lenape had come to depend on were becoming harder and harder to get. In the mid-18th century, under increasing pressure from expanding white settlements, and with their population severely reduced by repeated onslaughts of small pox, the Lenape were forced to move far westward onto the lands of their old friends the Wyondats, who themselves were late arrivals to the Ohio country. Also known as the Huron, the Wyondats had originally inhabited the north shore of Lake Ontario and the Georgian Bay area. Finding themselves on the losing end of a prolonged struggle with the Iroquois, they had fled southward, making Michigan and Ohio their new home.

Generations of close contact with both English and German settlers in eastern Pennsylvania had given the Lenape a knowledge of those European languages. By the time one of their bands had settled on the bluffs overlooking a small river on the western frontier the Lenape were also being significantly influenced by Moravian missionaries of German heritage. In naming their new village situated along an unnamed river the Indians chose European words that reflected these foreign influences. They attached "hell," the German word for "clear," to the English word "town" and thus the name Helltown was born. The name was not, as I had imagined, a derisive label attached to a site of decadency or sad degeneracy. It was simply a name describing the location of a new home located along a winding river of clear waters that would later be named the Clearfork Branch of the Mohican River.

The county history offered some fairly precise details identifying where the old Indian village had once been located along the Clearfork. The site was on a high bank, downstream from the town of Newville, and very near where Switzer Creek entered the river. Today the Clearfork flows toward Pleasant Hill Reservoir only a mile or so east of Malabar Farm. Switzer Creek flows through the heart of Malabar, and Newville is on State Route 95, only a couple miles south of Malabar Farm.

I began to wonder if I might be able to find Helltown. Not that I expected to discover any physical evidence of the Lenape after all these years. I simply wanted to stand upon the site and allow my imagination to travel back to their time, to hear the cawing of crows overhead as they might have heard them, to smell the earth and feel the breezes on my face as they had done, to walk the banks of the Clearfork following in their footsteps. Additional information written in the old history book further enhanced these musings. It was said that Captain Pipe had visited and possibly had even lived in Helltown for a time. Perhaps there was more to learn about this somewhat mythical figure and an amble through a portion of the world he inhabited might be a good place to start.

My hike into Lenape country began at Malabar Farm State Park in late December, the temperature in the tolerable mid-30s. As with four of the five hikes that form the core of this book, my "Indian" hike began by climbing the dirt lane that now takes Park visitors to Malabar Farm's Sugar Shack and Pugh Cabin. This lane was originally a part of the old Ferguson/Newville Road that in the nineteenth century led out of Pleasant Valley, crossed the surrounding ridges, and then dropped down into the village of Newville. The Ferguson Road and its namesake William Ferguson play a leading role in the next chapter, so I will save the telling of their story for later, and begin this tale where the old road crests the high and wooded hills that define the southern reaches of today's Malabar Farm State Park. On the level summit of the loftiest of these hills there is a broad open expanse known as the Ferguson Meadow. In *Pleasant Valley* Louis Bromfield tells of being able to see into three counties from this high vantage point. Today you can see only the sky above you, the grass at your feet, and the tall trees that surround the meadow, enclosing it with a luxuriant wall of brown and green. The meadow itself is kept free of the encroaching forest by periodically cutting the grasses. In the recent past golden brown "shredded wheat" hay bales that dotted this field in the summer.

My walk didn't immediately enter Ferguson Meadow itself, but followed along an undulating graveled lane through woods that parallel the northern side of the great field. The lane, about a half mile in length, terminates at a gas well, its small grassy opening encircled by the surrounding forest. When Louis Bromfield purchased the Herring Farm in 1939 the sale also included the old Ferguson Place high on the ridge top. At that time, there were two producing gas wells on the property, the original leases dating back to 1910. Bromfield heated his Big House and operated most of his kitchen appliances, including two refrigerators, with natural gas from his own land. I chose to walk this road not because it was easier to traverse than the meadow, but because traveling it always reminds me of one of my first hikes at Malabar. It was a cool springtime in the forenoon; the trees were just beginning to fill the sky with broad leaves that would soon form a dark green tunnel. Triangular shafts of soft morning sunlight slanted through the new leaves, illuminating the path with a patchwork of golden daubs. Bordering the lane on both sides was a proliferation of small flowering trees. White, four petal dogwood blossoms stood out in sharp relief against an understory that at the time still remained shrouded in vertical tones of dull brown and gray. Radiant with shifting dapples of sunlight, this flower-cloaked lane created an atmosphere that brought to mind Anne Shirley's poetic description of a blossoming apple orchard as her "White Way Delight" from Lucy Maude Montgomery's wonderful 1908 novel *Anne of Green Gables.*

Before reaching the gas well, which I really didn't want to see, its intruding presence an orange mechanical blemish on the surrounding forest, I turned onto the meadow, bisecting it on a portion of the Pleasant Valley Bridle Trail that circles the Park. Narrow and deeply cut into the turf by the hoofs of countless horses, this trail eventually re-enters the forest on the far south side of the meadow, where, about a hundred yards into the woods, there is an intersecting trail called the Pleasant Hill Loop. This loop serves as a link to connect Malabar's horseback riders and hikers with the extensive trail systems of both Pleasant Hill Reservoir and Mohican State Forest.

Ferguson Meadow itself is a welcoming place to spread a picnic blanket, especially in the late spring and early summer before the grasses have grown too high. Spring greens in a dozen tints and shades dominate the meadow floor, accented here and there by the yellow confetti of dandelions. Scattered randomly across the field are a dwindling number of ancient apple trees, their gnarled trunks clothed in splotches of pale green lichen. In springtime the aged and brittle branches of these trees still bring forth a surprising profusion of pink blossoms. The spicy aroma of honeysuckle wafts through the air on invisible currents and the sky overhead is a blithe canopy of cerulean blue. On this December day, however, the meadow was in a somber mood, shrouded by a low and cheerless blanket of gray clouds. At least it wasn't raining.

It had rained so heavily in recent days that the ground was saturated. The sunken bridle trail was filled with a slender, mirror-like pool of water that appeared as a thin slice of gray sky fallen to the earth. Crossing the open meadow exposed me to icy winter breezes. A cold chill ran up my arms and down my neck. Once more entering the shelter of the trees I quickly found the side trail that I expected would lead me into ancient Indian country. Being a relatively new trail, this loop, unlike much of the older bridle trail, had yet to be widened and muddied by horses. Here the footpath remained a narrow and inviting path, offering a pleasant stroll through a mixed forest of hardwoods and pines. The varied winter browns of assorted hardwoods, mixed with the dark shadows of red pines and the gray of scattered beech, offered my eyes only a limited palette of muted earth colors, but the ground at my feet was a plush carpet of newly fallen leaves, many of them still retaining traces of the reds, yellows, and oranges of late October. By December, green is a rare color in the woods. It was present here only as a pale memory, visible in dying grasses, in the long needles of red pines, and in the brighter evergreen of Christmas ferns. On this morning the ferns were still dusted with a sugary white coating of last night's light snowfall.

As it diverges from the bridle trail the Pleasant Hill Loop gradually turns southeast and away from the meadow. After passing through a stand of pines, the trail's northern flank drops away in a series of low steps until it reaches Switzer Creek. Emerging from the leaf strewn surface of this hillside are many gray sandstone outcroppings. Varying in width from a few feet to several dozen yards, their coarse lower edges are hidden behind tall ferns and grasses and their tops covered with a veneer of fallen leaves and small branches. These stones, rigid and unmoving, appear to grow directly out of the forest's floor and offer a striking contrast to the organic softness that surrounds them. With a modicum of imagination the larger stones begin to look like the arching backs of submerged whales, frozen in place upon the leaf strewn peaks and troughs of a brown and undulating sea. Almost lost among the larger outcroppings are the many smaller ones that appear to be rising only reluctantly out of the mottled earth of the forest floor.

If you walk the entire circle of the Pleasant Hill Loop Trail you will have traveled about three-quarters of a mile and you will find yourself back where you began, at the Pleasant Valley Bridle Trail near where it crosses Ferguson's Meadow.

However, half way around the loop a short connector trail continues to the east, linking Malabar Farm to Mohican State Forest and Pleasant Hill Reservoir. After descending a steep hillside this trail crosses State Route 95 and re-enters the forest. The plan of the day was to leave the loop at this connector. I would cross the highway and enter the low forested valley that had been sculpted by the Clearfork River. In this valley and along the Clearfork I hoped to find Helltown.

It is surprising how even on leafless winter days the forest can mask sounds. I was within a hundred yards of the highway before I began to detect the muffled rush of passing automobiles. Here, where the trail descends, a massive outcropping of sandstone, much larger than anything to be seen elsewhere along the Pleasant Hill Loop, grows out of the hillside. In the summer this great mass of stone is somewhat obscured by the luxuriant growth of summer foliage that covers the surrounding hills. However, in the barrenness of winter and the gray light of an overcast sky this coarsely textured rock stands out in a bold relief of yellow-ochre and rust colored sandstone. Diagonal layers of the hardened grains of sand are stacked one upon another in a textbook display of sedimentation. Thick mosses cling tightly to the many fissures that score the outcrop's lower surfaces. The varied greens of this moss contrast with the rich earth tones of the stone. Years ago an acorn became wedged into the debris filled crevice of an eroded sedimentary shelf on a lower side of this outcropping. Against all odds a tree sprouted. Resolute in its quest to find a secure purchase, the tiny sapling sent out coiling roots that slowly snaked their way down the rock's sandpaper surface, insinuating themselves into its many cracks. Although the effort has left its trunk stunted and its branches painfully twisted, the oak has survived, reaching skyward in a triumphant salute to the tenacity of life.

While briefly exploring the craggy upper surfaces of this outcropping I detected the faint gurgle of moving water. The sound appeared to be coming from the base of the rock, hidden beneath a broad overhanging ledge. Temporarily distracted from my primary objective, I left the trail. By grasping small trees to break my fall I inched slowly down and into a shallow, rock strewn ravine cut by a rivulet that flowed from an as yet unseen spring. Hand over hand, rock by boulder I followed the tumbling sparkle of rushing water upstream to its source beneath the mass of sandstone. I was rewarded for my efforts with the discovery of an enchanted Lilliputian world. The small stream cascaded, ledge by ledge, out of the gloomy depths of a deep and craggy fissure, a cavern in perfect miniature. Dark water instantly quickened to shimmering crystal as it cleared a low shelf and found daylight. Above this tiny cavern's yawning black mouth hung delicate strands of dripping moss. In the dampness along its edges, protected from the worst of winter's icy blasts, grew emerald clusters of watercress. Below the cave's watery entrance grew tight bunches of broad leafed grasses. A spray of small but hardy ferns, adorned with jewel-like droplets of ice water, added a regal presence to the scene. On any other day this tiny world would have been a destination in itself, but today I had a more pressing engagement in mind.

Climbing out of the rocky ravine and reclaiming the trail I descended to the highway. Standing at the road's edge I looked across and into the trees that pressed against its opposite berm. Several hundred yards behind me I had crossed the boundary separating Malabar Farm from land belonging to the Muskingum Watershed Conservancy and Pleasant Hill Reservoir. At my back lay a trail through the woods that continued uninterrupted to the pastures, fields and barns of Malabar Farm. Before me lay a world of a different sort. Switzer Creek passed through a culvert beneath the highway only a few hundred yards to my left. Helltown must lay only a half mile or so ahead, a short walk. At least that was what I believed at the time. I could see myself crossing the highway and stepping back in time, back to the days of the Lenape, back to the world of Captain Pipe and Onalsaka.

Surely, Lenape hunters and warriors had ranged far and wide through the surrounding landscape, had refreshed themselves at the spring high above me, and had trekked over the forested hills and valleys that now make up Malabar Farm. I could picture these men following the banks of Switzer Creek upstream for miles in search of wild game. In my mind's eye I imagined that after I crossed the narrow strip of concrete I would be standing on their soil, on Lenape home ground. This simple act would make the world of Captain Pipe a little bit closer, a little bit more tangible. A narrow swath of gray, with a yellow line running down its middle, was all that separated me from what I fancifully imagined to be the haunt of ancient Indians.

Like so much of American history, Captain Pipe's story has been buried beneath the clutter of time and neglect, lost among the exciting tales of more "significant" people and more "important" events. All too often the neglected men and women of our past, the individuals like Captain Pipe, have become little more than fallen and forgotten leaves on the family tree of our collective national history. If acknowledged at all they are thought of as sideline participants, helpless souls carried along on a swirling current of events far beyond their understanding or ability to control. Although their exploits have for the most part been forgotten, many of these individuals were, in fact, quite active players in the making of those streams that defined critical events, streams that elevated other individuals to historic prominence. In clearing away the dust that blanketed Captain Pipe's story I came to understand that his life was played out along the margins of two opposing categories, the famous and the forgotten. Incongruous as it sounds he was both a co-pilot and an unwilling passenger on the greater ship of American history. It is an undeniable truth that Pipe's people were rudely swept aside by the westward expansion of an alien culture that was beyond their ability to successfully resist. Captain Pipe did not, however, go quietly into the night. He was actively involved in the steering of many of those powerful events that shaped our nation's early history. He did indeed have an influence on the story of the dramatic end of the Ohio wilderness and the ultimate settlement of that frontier by men not of his race or color.

His real name was Komesch-quano-heel, "Maker of Light," but the Lenape also called him Hopocan "Pipe Tobacco." White settlers knew him as Captain Pipe. He was born into the Wolf Clan of the Lenape sometime around 1725, probably somewhere along the banks of the Susquehanna River in Pennsylvania. Not much is known of his childhood, but his early years were most likely spent in the village of his uncle, the Lenape chief Custaloga. Custaloga's main village was located on French Creek in Crawford County near present day Meadville, Pennsylvania. The first written record of Captain Pipe comes in 1759, when he appears in colonial records among the warriors at a conference at Fort Pitt, called by the British to secure an alliance with the Lenape during the French and Indian War. In that same year he was recorded as being responsible for marking the boundaries of land on the Tuscarawas River near present day Bolivar, Ohio. Captain Pipe also was among the Lenape present at Fort Pitt conferences in 1765 and 1768. By 1773 he had succeeded his uncle Custaloga as chief.

The outbreak of the American Revolutionary War caused much internal strife and discord among the many Indian nations. The war split the powerful Iroquois Confederation, pitting tribe against tribe as the Indians fought to secure their precarious standing with either the British or the Americans. Captain Pipe desperately tried to keep his followers neutral, seeing nothing but grief for his own people should they lend their support to either side. He continued to pursue this position even after American troops, failing to distinguish between friendly and hostile tribes, attacked one of his villages in 1778, killing his mother, a brother, and several of his children. In that same year, in a request openly dismissive of Lenape efforts to remain neutral despite their grieving over murdered relatives, American general Lachlin

McIntosh asked the Lenape for permission to take his army through their land on a campaign to attack the British at Fort Detroit. Captain Pipe convinced the Lenape to allow this after the Americans promised to build and staff a fort to defend the Lenape against any possible British reprisals. Fort Laurens was constructed near the Lenape villages in east central Ohio. Not content with this limited cooperation, General McIntosh soon followed it with a demand upon the Lenape that would have deadly repercussions far beyond the general's imagining. McIntosh insisted that the Indians join him on his march on Detroit or face extinction from the guns of his soldiers. Believing the Americans to be weaker than they claimed, Captain Pipe and fellow Lenape chiefs turned to the British, offering to ally with them, though no immediate alliance was concluded.

Once they had turned to the British, Captain Pipe abandoned his village on the Tuscarawas and relocated to what he thought would be a more secure site on the Walhonding River south of present day Coshoctan, Ohio. In 1781 American Colonel Daniel Brodhead attacked and destroyed this village, killing a number of Indians in the process. This may have been the same Captain Broadhead whose men that same year are said to have fired upon Pipe's relatives, killing his sister as she stood atop a sandstone cliff in Pleasant Valley. In any event the attack on the Walhonding village was the final act that would drive Captain Pipe and his people to initiate a formal coalition with the British. Pipe and his surviving followers moved to the banks of Tymochtee Creek near the Sandusky River. The village he established there became known as Pipe's Town. Captain Pipe would remain on Tymochtee Creek for the duration of the war, trying unsuccessfully to thwart American advances westward. In 1782 he helped defeat Colonel Crawford's punitive Ohio expedition against hostile Indian tribes. Crawford, a veteran of the French and Indian War, had retired from the military in 1781. The following year he was persuaded to don his uniform again and lead a campaign against the threat of hostile Indians along the

Sandusky River. At the head of an army of 500 volunteers Crawford hoped to surprise the Indians. Unknown to the Colonel the British and their Indian allies at Fort Detroit had learned of his plan. Some 450 Indians rushed to the Sandusky, where they waited in ambush. In a surprise attack Crawford's force was routed and his men sent fleeing for their lives. Colonel Crawford was captured, along with many of his men.

This battle had followed close on the heels of the massacre of nearly one-hundred innocent Christian Indians; men, women, and children at the Moravian Mission called Gnadenhutten. Gnadenhutten is a German word meaning "cabins of grace." but it was far from a scene of grace on March 8, 1782. Pennsylvania militia from Pittsburgh, seeking revenge for raids in Pennsylvania, herded non-resisting Mission Indians into cabins and then, taking their prisoners out two-by-two, had brutally bludgeoned them to death. In all, twenty-eight men, twenty-nine women and thirty-nine children died. Only two young boys escaped, one of them scalped, to tell of the murders. It was a sad example of extremely poor timing on the part of the Indians of Gnadenhutten. They had arrived at the Mission only days before the Militia's arrival.

The Mission of Gnadenhutten had been established by the Moravian Brethren in 1772 and was one of six such settlements built along the Tuscarawas River in the 1770s. The Indians who lived at these missions were steeped in the Moravian doctrine of non-violence, and soon found themselves caught between opposing forces during the American Revolution. In 1781 Gnadenhutten was plundered by a band of Indians allied to the British. The Christian Lenape living there were rounded up and incarcerated at "Captive Town" on the Sandusky River. Held in near concentration camp conditions during a particularly harsh winter the captives were slowly starving. In February of 1782 they were allowed to return to the Gnadenhutten Mission, where they hoped to save any corn still standing in their abandoned fields. Only days after their return to the Mission they were discovered and killed by the vengeful militia from Pennsylvania.

In retaliation for this brutal massacre of the innocent Gnadenhutten Indians the enraged Indians who held Colonel Crawford captive smudged his face with charcoal, a symbolic act that marked him for torture and death, despite the fact that Crawford had had no culpability in the Mission murders. His cruel and barbarous death has been recorded elsewhere in considerable detail. Captain Pipe's possible participation in Crawford's death, however, is less well documented. Some Indians later claimed that it was Captain Pipe himself who applied the charcoal to Colonel Crawford's forehead.

Captain Pipe continued his resistance to settlers invading his Ohio country even after the end of the Revolutionary War. However, by the beginning of the second decade of the nineteenth century he had concluded that the Lenape couldn't halt the advancing whites. He entered into negotiations with the government that resulted in treaties defining what lands would remain in Indian hands. Though they were in blatant violation of these treaties, the army of white settlers that flooded into Ohio at the conclusion of the War of 1812 soon negated Pipe's best efforts. In the years that followed, he and his people became wanderers, residing in various locations across northeastern and central Ohio. Finally pushed beyond their ability to endure, the Lenape left the Ohio country forever, eventually settling near the present site of Orestes, Indiana. Even there they found no permanent respite. The Treaty of St. Mary's in 1818 threatened the Indians with forced removal if they didn't leave on their own within three years. In 1821 the Lenape left for Kansas, but Pipe was no longer leading them. He had died in 1818 at the age of about 94, shortly after arriving in Indiana.

The trail beyond the highway soon widened into a muddy quagmire, lined on both sides by thorny multi-flora rose. I had no

choice but to plunge into the oozing mess, mud clinging more heavily to my boots with each step. Fortunately after a few hundred feet, the trail narrowed and the mud lessened. My plan was to follow this path until I came to Switzer Creek. I would then follow the creek downstream to where it emptied into the Clearfork River. At that point all that would be required to locate the approximate site of Helltown would be to follow the river upstream a couple of hundred yards. Unfortunately, as they say about best laid plans, it didn't turn out to be quite that simple, and it was my own fault. At home I had an aerial photograph of the Malabar/Pleasant Hill area, with the trails overlaying the picture. If I had consulted that map beforehand, or better yet, if I had brought the map with me, the confusion that was to come could easily have been avoided. Lesson learned, if traveling in
a new and unfamiliar area take a map, even if you think you know where you are going. In any event the hike was a good one, though it did turn out to be somewhat longer and more challenging than I had first planned.

The western side of the Clearfork River is low bottom land, and from what I had heard previously is damp much of the year. In the summer it is the perfect breeding ground for insects of every description, especially mosquitoes. I soon discovered that it is also the perfect country for water loving sycamore trees. They flourish here, their mottled greenish-white trunks standing out like Greek columns across the forest landscape. Today their white branches etched crisp lines against a charcoal sky, a calligraphic display of mother-nature's own unique script. One of the easiest trees to identify, the sycamore, also known as the buttonwood, is one of my favorite trees in the forest. I like the unique texture of its exfoliating bark, its distinctive white color, and its broad parchment-like leaves. I especially enjoy the way the sycamore contrasts with the dark browns and grays of other trees. In winter you can often trace the course of a distant and unseen stream by following the zig-zag line of ghostly white sycamores lining its banks. In the spring sycamores can be tapped for their sweet sap, but the amount of sugar in the sap is much less than that of sugar maples and, therefore, the tapping of sycamores is not a commercially productive venture. In emergency situations, however, tapping a sycamore will provide a source of pure and slightly sweet water. Our American sycamore probably received its name from early colonists who noted its resemblance to the English sycamore maple.

While pausing for a few silent moments to enjoy the sycamores that surrounded me my eye caught movement off to my right. There, almost lost in thick underbrush, maybe two hundred feet away, was an elderly gentleman in hunting camouflage holding not a gun but a metal detector, which was a good thing since it wasn't hunting season. I really don't like coming upon strangers unexpectedly in the woods, especially if they are carrying a gun, hunting season or not. The old man was swinging the detector back and forth in a slow arc, intently studying the ground at his feet. I don't think he was even aware of my presence. At first I thought to leave him to his work, but curiosity got the better of me. I approached him slowly and announced myself with a "hello" that I hoped wouldn't startle him. "I apologize for bothering you, I didn't expect to see anyone else in these woods. I was just curious, what do you hope to find out here?" Continuing to swing his detector as he spoke, the old man gave me a brief outline history of the area.

It seems that this place where I was walking, this bottom land of mud, bugs and sycamores, had once been populated by settlers who had cleared the forest and farmed the flat land. The last of the homesteads had been removed during the 1930s when the Army Corp of Engineers built Pleasant Hill Reservoir for flood control. This entire area was declared within the flood plain for the new lake, precipitating its forced evacuation. This was the same declaration that would also doom the town of Newville. The old fellow then pointed out a rectangular depression in the ground, the remains of a cellar that I had completely overlooked.

My attention was also directed toward an old road, its slightly sunken route now mostly lost under thick brush and trees. He had hoped to find some artifacts from the early years, coins and such, but wasn't having much luck. The trash of recent years was getting in his way. Looking around I saw what he meant. Mixed in with the duff of the forest floor was a profusion of half buried beer cans, pop cans, and plastic bottles that I hadn't noticed before. I also learned that this locale, being a convenient convergence of road, a river, and a reservoir, was a popular spot for fishermen. The abundance of discarded trash suggested strongly that many of these "sportsmen" lacked much of an environmental consciousness. Unfortunately, I was to see more of this cast off waste as I continued my hike.

Not wishing to bother the old gentleman further I thanked him for his time and left him to his searching. Back on the trail I soon came to the ford where the bridle trail crosses Switzer Creek. It was just as well that I had not planned to cross the creek here because the trail plunged down a muddy embankment and directly into a churning current of brown water, much wider and moving much faster than I had expected. Between Malabar Farm and here the creek had picked up a considerable amount of additional water, and it was hurrying past me at great speed on its way to join the Clearfork. A faint fisherman's trail ran parallel to the creek and I turned to follow it downstream. The rushing water snaked its way through the woods, cutting deeply into its outer bank with each turn. At one sharp bend the relentless current had so completely undermined the roots of a cottonwood that it had collapsed. As it fell across the creek the upper portion of its trunk had landed on the opposite bank, forming a natural bridge. A seine of smaller branches was left dangling in the stream to capture passing debris in a slow dam-building process that one day would likely alter the creek's course. At another more gently arcing bend further downstream the creek's current had scoured out a wide expanse of sandy, pebble strewn beach. The wet sand held the footprints of several deer, at least one raccoon, and a number of tiny, unidentified forest creatures. I added my prints to the mix, knowing that all would be swept away during the next big rain.

Much of the creek's edge beyond this sandy washout was matted with dead grasses that made the walking easy. A narrow and much used animal trail cut a line perpendicular to my own path and entered the stream in a slick mud chute. I followed the trail back from the water about fifteen feet to where it disappeared into a six inch hole in the ground. Beaver will sometimes live in holes dug deep into the banks of waterways, but this hole was a considerable distance from the water. Anyway, it seemed far too small for a beaver, and there were no beaver gnawed trees to be seen in the surrounding area. Perhaps it was the home of a muskrat? While muskrats are partial to marshes and ponds, they will also inhabit streams and rivers. Like the beaver, a muskrat will build lodges or live in burrows, but unlike the beaver, muskrats do not build dams. The burrows of muskrats, like those of river beaver, are usually built into muddy banks, with an entrance six or more inches below water. That didn't fit with the location of my burrow. Could it be the home of a mink? Mink are equally comfortable in stream, pond, and on land. Though rarely seen they survive successfully even when they share habitat with human populations.

It would have been interesting to set up a blind and wait patiently for the hole's owner to return to or emerge from his hole, but I had neither the inclination nor the time for that. As an interesting aside, the mink, though it can't spray like a skunk, discharges a liquid from an anal musk gland that is just as foul smelling. The mink's name comes from the Swedish word *menk,* meaning "the stinking creature from Finland". I'm guessing that there might be some cultural prejudice being vented here. The name muskrat comes from the Algonquian word *musquash.*

As I continued my walk downstream the woods began to open up and the leaden sky grow more pronounced against a thinning filigree of bare branches overhead. Suddenly the trees disappeared and I found myself facing a broad and satiny sheet of gray mud occupying the space where I had expected a forest. Several hundred yards to my left the mud melted into a thin slice of silvery water that itself quickly dissolved into the smoky blue

Switzer Creek cutting its way toward the Clearfork River.

background of what had to be the hills encircling Pleasant Hill Reservoir. Switzer Creek emptied into this sea of mud, becoming a slender ribbon of brown as it cut across the gray flatness and curved gracefully toward the distant lake. To my right the mud extended several hundred yards, ending in a sweeping line of trees. Surprised as I was, having expected to find Switzer Creek entering the Clearfork, what disturbed me most was what I saw in front of me. Before me, across four or five hundred feet of mud was a low line of trees backed by a high and very steep hill. Where was the river? How could I have missed it? How would I find the location of Helltown if I couldn't even discover where Switzer Creek merged with the Clearfork River? Switzer Creek now seemed to be moving across an open expanse of mud in the general direction of a river that wasn't there. From my vantage point it seemed that at best the creek would eventually empty into the distant lake. However, the river had to be around here somewhere; the Clearfork was the river that had been dammed in the 1930s to create Pleasant Hill Reservoir. I was so confounded by the expanse of mud confronting me that I have to admit I wasn't thinking logically at that moment. All I could think to do was retrace my steps, start over again, and look for the river elsewhere. How that would help me find Helltown I wasn't sure. I had previously established a GPS way-point at the site of the town of Newville, but now a GPS reading from the spot where Switzer Creek entered the mud flat placed me only a mile downstream from Newville, more than a half mile short of where the old history book said Helltown had been located relative to that later community. If the book was accurate, if Helltown was a mile and a half downstream from Newville, then that would place the Indian village yet another a half mile to my left and now quite possibly lost beneath the waters of the reservoir. If, as also claimed in the book, the village had been situated on a bluff overlooking the river, then it seemed possible that the site might yet remain above water, but it would be visible only from the vantage point of a boat on the lake. This was a very discouraging thought. Not only had I somehow lost an entire river, but even if I did manage to find the Clearfork, it seemed likely that the waters of the reservoir would make it impossible for me to locate Helltown. The work of the Army Corp of Engineers would prevent me from completing my quest.

I quickly retraced my steps back along Switzer Creek, past the mysterious hole in the ground, past the footprints pressed into wet sand, past the cottonwood bridge, back to the point where I had turned away from the bridle trail to follow the creek. Sitting down on an old log that had fallen parallel to the stream, I began to ponder the situation. I had not come this far only to give up now. I knew that the river had to be out there somewhere. If I turned into the woods at an angle that slanted diagonally southeast, and if I kept walking long enough, then surely I would find it. Rising from the log, I turned my back to the stream and walked into the woods. I couldn't imagine the river being more than a half mile distant. Once I located it I would be able to follow it downstream to where it emptied into the lake. At that point I should be able to orient myself relative to Newville, Switzer Creek, the Clearfork River, and Pleasant Hill Reservoir. What this would mean with reference to finding Helltown, however, I didn't know.

The going was now a little more difficult than it had been along the creek. I found myself skirting impenetrable patches of multi-flora rose and circling around several long, low and water filled depressions that looked very much like old abandoned roadways. I even came across a moss covered pile of stones that appeared to have been cut into rough block shapes. Perhaps this was evidence of a long gone homestead, although I couldn't find a cellar depression. At the very least this pile of rocks was evidence of someone's hard labor long ago as he cleared a field for planting. Despite these detours I eventually found myself standing on the banks of what I was sure had to be the Clearfork, though the current was very sluggish and the river wider than I had expected. The water's flow, crawling along as did, was at least moving in the correct direction. I further reasoned that perhaps it was wider than I expected because of all the heavy rains of recent days. Switzer Creek had also been wider than I had thought it should to be. As I emerged from the cover of the trees I startled a great blue heron that had been wading near the water's edge below me. Quickly lifting into the air, the big bird's long wings beat out a slow and graceful rhythm as it noiselessly disappeared into a dense line of trees further downstream.

All that I had to do now was follow the river downstream to discover how I had missed it earlier. Easy, or so I imagined. I followed the river's lazy current for several long minutes, crawling over and under blow-downs and dodging more thickets of multi-flora rose. Along the way I came upon another of my favorite trees, the burr oak. I have long admired oaks in general, but the burr, because I encounter it so infrequently on my walks, has always been special. To me oak trees speak of true wildness. Their acorns provide a rich store of nature's bounty, depended upon by many forest creatures, both great and small. For native peoples the oak, especially the white oak, was a vital part of their diet. The acorn of the white oak, pounded into a rough meal, was a primary ingredient in the hard dry bread baked by many tribes. In their mature years, oaks, survivors by then of countless howling winds and lightning storms, stand proud and enduring. From their aged and knotty trunks grow muscular, gnarled branches, arms that time and the elements have twisted into strange and grotesque forms, the likes of which are rarely seen elsewhere in the forest. It is no wonder that these fantastical giants of the woodlands played such an important role in the religious practices of Druid priests who worshiped in special oak groves.

In the fall, the high tannin content in oak leaves slows the decaying process and gives them their rich russet color. Throughout the long months of winter these leaves cling to their branches much more tenaciously than do those of most other deciduous trees. In this obstinate possessiveness the oak is second only to the even more doggedly stubborn beech. On tranquil winter days, when the darkening shadows of evening slowly descend upon the forest floor, soft breezes announce their arrival and the lofty branches of tall oaks are set to gently swaying. In a symbiotic relationship as old as time, invisible currents join with dry parchment leaves. Together they begin to whisper in subtle timbres, giving voice to an ancient and lyric tongue. Gradually, the rustlings become more articulate, offering up hushed and primeval narratives of things and times beyond conscious memory, things of the spirit, things perhaps even eternal. Thus it is that the forest of today speaks the same ageless language that two thousand years ago stirred the Druids' imagination.

Please indulge me as I briefly digress to write a little more of some trees that I have come to know on my many forest walks. The shagbark hickory, easily recognizable by its coarsely textured trunk of peeling bark, stands resolute in its wild nature. Shagbarks produce a nut that, like the acorn, is an important wildlife staple. The name hickory comes from the Algonquian word "pawcohiccora," referring to the tree's oily nut, an important source of food for many Indian tribes. Also popular as a fuel for smoking meat, the shagbark hickory resides at number three on the hierarchy of my favorite hardwood trees, behind only the oak and the sycamore. With apologies to our Canadian neighbors to the north, as well as those in Vermont, maple trees seem to be at risk of losing their wild edge. Although maples do grow abundantly in many deciduous forests, they also grace far more suburban lawns than do any other species of tree. In October the maple does for a few short weeks unleash the suppressed side of its wild character. Reveling in a brief but extravagant display of narcissistic self-expression, the maple pushes aside all other trees as it paints itself and the surrounding countryside in a hundred different shades of orange and scarlet. In February and March, however, the maple returns once again to its domesticated station. In that season it passively submits to the cultivated practice of tapping, the sacrificing of its sweet sap to make the maple syrup that will soon thereafter be poured over countless plates of breakfast hotcakes. Having expressed my impressions concerning the Janus nature of maple trees, I must admit to holding a certain abiding affection for them. Domesticated or wild, sugar, red, or silver, it matters little, the maple rests secure at number four on my list of favorite trees.

In declaring my appreciation for the oak, the hickory, the sycamore, and with some reservations, the maple, I must acknowledge that there is also a dark side to my feelings concerning certain trees. The black cherry, for example, has fallen far out of my favor. The black cherry has a very thin canopy. This tree, where it occurs in numbers, permits far too much sunlight to reach the forest floor, severely reducing the moisture content required of a healthy hardwood forest. Unfortunately the black cherry is a favorite of furniture makers and the timber industry, who love it for its beautiful fine grained reddish brown wood. Two hundred years ago the number of black cherry trees in most hardwood forests didn't exceed perhaps 3 or 4% of the total trees present. Now, to the detriment of the long term viability of affected forests, the black cherry is encouraged to multiply in quantities far in excess of what would occur in a natural woodland environment. In some "managed" forests the black cherry accounts for nearly 35% of all trees. Beautiful though its wood may be, the black cherry has become an industrial tree, a victim of commercial exploitation, having lost both its wild forest personality and a certain untamed dignity.

As a final nod to my favorite trees I have to acknowledge the black walnut. As with the black cherry, the black walnut has long been exploited for its rich dark wood, used in everything from fine furniture to gun stocks and flooring. Despite this commercial association the black walnut remains at heart a wild tree. Relatively rare in closed forests, it needs full sunlight to thrive. It is more at home in riparian environments, and is common along the borders of many open fields. In addition to its wood, the hard shell of the black walnut nut is used commercially in abrasives, and strange as it sounds, in cosmetics. Its nutmeat is also harvested as a food ingredient. Fortunately the black walnut nutmeat isn't as sweet as that of the more widely cultivated English walnut, or by now it might also have lost its wild character. The black walnut comes in at number five on my list of favorite hardwoods.

It wasn't long before my hike down the Clearfork began to disconnect from my expectations. My river seemed to be coming to an end in a mud flat, narrowing abruptly to a four foot wide channel leisurely threading its way through thick gray muck. Looking around I could see no forking of the river's flow, no other place for the water to go. Clearly this slender thread of water cutting through ooze wasn't the Clearfork. The river was still missing! Peering through thinning trees I could see into the far horizon and an open field of gray, and a low, scrubby tree line that seemed somehow familiar. Slowly it began to dawn on my now somewhat befuddled mind that the field of gray opening to my front was the same broad mud flat that had confounded me earlier, the same mud that had ended my walk down Switzer Creek, the same sheet of gray that had sent me retracing my steps back up the creek to begin again in a new direction. Not only had I once more failed to find the Clearfork, I had simply traveled in a big circle. With nothing constructive coming to mind to guide my actions I headed for the familiar, for the mud that had become my nemesis. In minutes I was back at the banks of Switzer Creek, back at the edge of the sweeping mud flat, staring at footprints that I had made only an hour earlier. Confused and not a little discouraged, I pondered my next move.

It was time to pause and think, time to sort all of this out. First there was the problem of the GPS reading. My GPS unit showed a distance of about a mile between Newville and where I now stood. The 1908 history of the county had told me that a mile and a half separated Newville and Helltown. This would place the Helltown site yet another half mile downriver, assuming the river, though as yet undiscovered, was nearby. Based on this thinking, the village lay somewhere beneath the waters of the reservoir, or if still on dry land, then accessible from my position only by boat. On the other hand, I had to be somewhere near the confluence of Switzer Creek and the Clearfork, even if I had yet to find the Clearfork.

The same 1908 history identified the Indian village as being a few hundred yards upstream from where the creek flowed into the river. How to account for this apparent discrepancy of half a mile? Was Helltown truly lost to me under Pleasant Hill Reservoir, or was there still a chance to find it if I could only discover where creek and river met, assuming of course that I could even find the river. I reasoned that more than a hundred years ago, when the mileage estimate between Newville and Helltown was originally established, there were no satellites and therefore no GPS technology. The mileage between the two sites was probably based on someone following the Clearfork downstream, someone who perhaps had included the winding route of the river in his estimate. Certainly the irregular course of the river could add a half mile to his measurement. All of this assumed that that original measurement had even been that carefully calculated in the first place, and was not simply an educated guess on someone's part. The problem of distances thus tentatively resolved I began to hope that I might yet find Helltown, and it might be quite near, if only I could find the Clearfork.

The mud flat was obviously the exposed floor of the upper end of the reservoir, revealed now because the water level had been lowered for the winter. In summer all of this expanse of flat, gray land would be covered by the lake. The strange body of slowly moving water that I had come upon earlier had to be the remnants of a muddy backwater, a depressed area cut off from the main body of the reservoir as the lake's level was lowered. The only outlet for this isolated pool of water was a slender, laggardly flowing passage across an ash-gray mire. In the summer this backwater would define the shallow and marshy southern reaches of the reservoir. Its muddy shoreline would become a dense, green and swampy place where great blue herons could fish undisturbed.

Before me, across the expanse of mud, and laying in mocking repose, was the line of low scraggly trees I had observed earlier. Could they be willows? Weren't willows often found in wetlands and along streams and rivers? Could the Clearfork be flowing out of sight just beyond those trees, sandwiched between them and the steep bank that rose so near to their back? I considered that I might circle back to where I had recently disturbed the heron. By walking further to the southwest I could pass beyond the furthest reaches of the backwater that I had foolishly confused with the Clearfork. Walking to the east from there I would surely discover the river. All that I needed to do then was follow it back to these distant willow trees. This would take time, however, and both my energy and the afternoon were waning. There seemed to be only one quick and sure way left open to me. I would have to cross the mud. With so much time already invested I didn't want my quest for Helltown to end in a complete debacle, but was challenging the mud a sensible alternative, was it even safe?

Several sets of deer tracks crossed the mud, indicating that they had made the passage safely. There were no carcasses or surface disturbances to suggest that any deer, having become stuck and unable to extricate itself, had starved to death or sunk beneath the muddy surface. I didn't weigh that much more than an adult deer. If a deer could pass safely surely I could too. Following in the tracks of a deer, and using my walking stick as a probe, I took my first tentative steps into the muck. I have walked through mud many times before, but this was different. Each footstep was a challenge, with viscid clay pulling against my boots like a giant suction cup. Lift one leg and squish it down, lift the other and do the same. The mud clung tenaciously to my boots, and was soon crawling up my pant legs. Fortunately with each stride I was only sinking in three or four inches, it could have been much worse. The flat cheerless surface that surrounded me was matted with decaying leaves, black against the monotone gray of the muck. Here and there ancient tree stumps, frozen in time, poked boney fingers up through the drab slime. Half buried beer cans and pop bottles lay all about, the debris of many a thoughtless boater I supposed. During half of the year shallow waters cover this ground. This upper end of the reservoir is frequented primarily by fishermen who apparently are of the opinion that empty beer cans are too heavy to haul out.

About half way across the gummy lake bed, and surrounded as I was by a flat expanse of thick mud, a series of dark and disturbing thoughts crept into my mind. What if I stepped into a hidden depression and sank in up to my knees, or even up to my hips? I would be trapped in the middle of a wide expanse of mud, unable to extricate myself, who would know of my plight? What if my phone didn't work from here? Even if it did work how embarrassed would I be calling for help? What if I went in deeper than my hips? A vision of only my stocking cap left to join the rotting leaves on the muddy surface forced its way into my consciousness. It is amazing how quickly such a series of grim thoughts can insinuate themselves into one's thinking. I was, however, already at mid-point in the crossing. I reasoned that it would be a terrible waste of effort and energy to turn back now, thus leaving any hope of finding Helltown lost in the mud at my feet. So, shaking off black thoughts of calamity, I forged ahead and without incident finally made it to the far side of the flat and to the line of scraggly willows.

I stepped up and over a low, undercut embankment, my boots thickly plastered with pasty gray mud, my lower pant legs encrusted with a whitish opaque powder where the mud has already begun to dry. Moving into the thin line of low trees I found dry earth, loose, sandy, and matted heavily with the dead grasses of last fall, but solid ground nonetheless. Many of the surrounding trees appeared broken and lifeless, stretching crooked branches skyward as if in unfulfilled supplication. I passed quickly beyond these sad trees, and thanking the gods who seemingly had forsaken them, I found the river. There it was, a brown ribbon of rushing water pressed tightly against the opposite bluff. It was right where I hoped it would be. Squeezed as it was into the narrow passage that lay between the willows and the bluff, the swiftly flowing river was surprisingly quiet, in spite of the hurry with which it sped toward Pleasant Hill Reservoir. Relieved that I had finally found the Clearfork I also felt a little foolish that it had taken so long.

A more reasoned consideration of reservoirs and water level management would have helped me interpret the reservoir's inlet environment better. A closer look at my aerial map of the area before embarking on my adventure would have accomplished much the same thing. Examining the map after the fact clearly revealed the narrow and hooked stretch of backwater that I had mistaken for the river. Analyzing its shape and location I concluded that this pool was probably the remnant of a former channel of the river. So, in a manner of speaking, I had discovered the river when I first came upon this pool, just not the river of today. The map clearly showed where the Clearfork pressed tightly against a steep hillside before reaching the lake. The photograph, taken in the summer, also showed Switzer Creek emptying into the upper reaches of Pleasant Hill Reservoir, rather than into the river. As I said above, this enlightening observation was, however, made only well after the fact. On this day, by turning to my left and looking down river, I could see the thin silver line of the creek cutting through the mud just beyond a point where the willows ended in a sand bar. The stream widened and flattened into a miniature delta as it crossed the final few yards of mud and sand to empty itself into the river. The wide, horizontal achromatic plane of the reservoir lay visible only a short distance beyond where Switzer Creek met the Clearfork River.

I followed the river the few dozen yards downstream to where Switzer entered it. Looking back across the mud flat and the creek's distinct snake-like path across it, I was struck by a revelation that would have come much sooner had I studied my map. Earlier in the year, when the reservoir's level would be much higher, Switzer Creek wouldn't be found flowing into the Clearfork River as it was today. It would be flowing into the reservoir itself at the very spot where I had originally been confounded by the mud flat. If the level of the reservoir had not been lowered for the season I wouldn't have been able to so easily stand where I was now. I would have been standing in at least several feet of water. In the summer a hike to find Helltown by reckoning from where the creek and the river came together would have been impossible. In that season the two would never meet. By dumb luck alone I had chosen the best time of the year to search for Helltown. From this perspective I considered that, in the years and decades past, Switzer Creek would still have flowed into the Clearfork somewhere near where I now stood. All I had to do was follow the river upstream several hundred yards and I should be about as close to the location of old Lenape village as I was going to get.

I found the muddy edges of the river to be somewhat firmer ground than the lake bed had been and moved upstream quickly, counting off several hundred wide footsteps. The bluff across the river from where I stopped counting paces was steep, its uppermost reaches some thirty to forty feet above the river. The nearly vertical slope of the bluff was composed primarily of a dull, yellowish clay, studded here and there with boulders and a scattering of small pines that struggled to maintain a grip on the steep incline. Along its top edge the bluff was guarded by a dark and mixed formation of evergreens and leafless hardwoods. The county history book that had provided me the approximate location of Helltown relative to Switzer Creek also described it as on a hillside overlooking the river. I wondered, would the Indians establish a village at a location with such an abrupt and precarious drop to water? I didn't believe they would, so I walked a little further upstream to where the bluff began a gradual descent toward the water. Here grasses grew and trees found better purchase; here village inhabitants would have had relatively easy access to river, and yet would have been secure from the ravages

Clearfork River, bordered by high bluffs.

of flood waters during heavy rains. Here was where I decided Helltown had once stood. Looking across the river and into the distant trees I could imagine the angular and indistinct forms of small cabins; I could visualize thin threads of white smoke rising from many cooking fires, their wispy lines twisting lazily skyward through the trees. I could see dark haired women dressed in colorful trade cloth, clay pots under each arm, carefully picking their way down a narrow path to the water's edge.

Helltown had been founded sometime in the mid-18th century, soon after the Lenape had been pushed out of their ancestral homelands far to the east in what is now eastern Pennsylvania and New Jersey. Unfortunately, they hadn't found enduring security in their new home. Helltown was abandoned in 1782, the Indians fleeing in fear when they got word of the massacre of fellow Lenape at Gnadenhutten. Some of them fled to their Wyondot friends at Upper Sandusky; others joined a company of white men led by Thomas Green, a character of some disrepute who had participated in the bloody massacre of over 200 American soldiers at the Wyoming battle of 1778. As late as

1881, a hundred years after its abandonment, a number of Lenape graves still existed at the site of Helltown, but within a few more years farmers had plowed them under. Excavation a decade or two later uncovered a few iron knives, an iron tomahawk, and some stone arrowheads, but nothing else remained. Imagine the indignation and uproar that would result today if a farmer were to plow up a pioneer cemetery. I wonder at the reasoning that says it is alright to plunder or destroy a burial ground as long as it isn't a part of one's own culture and history. Such a profound violation of another's heritage, demonstrated with such utter disrespect for the graves of Helltown, is becoming a growing issue among many Native American tribes. Were a few additional acres of corn or wheat that important to those late nineteenth century farmers? Are we behaving differently today? Are twenty-first century universities and museums to be excused for desecrating ancient graves in the name of research?

Together with Thomas Green's renegade whites, the Helltown Indians built the town of Greentown on the banks of the Black Fork River, about six miles northeast of the Helltown site, and about two miles north of the present town of Perrysville, Ohio. Greentown, with some 150 dwellings and a longhouse measuring 25 feet by 60 feet, was an important Indian town on the Pittsburgh-Sandusky Trail until 1812, when its Indian inhabitants were temporarily imprisoned and the town burned by soldiers who feared that the Indians would use the disruptions of the War of 1812 as an opportunity to remedy old grievances. Ironically the destruction of Greentown actually precipitated the Indian attacks so feared by the whites. One of the most notable of these attacks occurred on September 15, 1812 only a few miles from Greentown.

On Mifflin Township Road 1225 in Ashland County a small monument stands, dedicated to what has come to be known as the Copus massacre. The Reverend James Copus was an early settler in the area, having arrived in 1809. Living near Greentown,

The dedication of the Copus Monument, 1882

The Copus Monument today.
photograph courtesy Malabar Farm State Park

he often visited the village as a missionary and had always been on friendly terms with the Indians. At the beginning of the War of 1812 the United States military asked the Reverend to speak with the Indians and persuade them, for their own safety, to relocate for the duration of the war. Copus was at first disinclined to help, perhaps being skeptical of the military's stated intentions, but he was eventually convinced to cooperate when warned that if the

63

Indians didn't leave "blood would flow." Copus went to Greentown, and being trusted by the Indians, convinced them that for their own security they should make the move. He also assured them that their property would be protected and that they would be able to return to their homes when the danger of war had passed. Though loath to leave their village the Indians took Copus at his word and agreed to a temporary relocation.

The Reverend's initial reservations had been well founded. He had been deceived. The truth of the matter was that the army was concerned that the Greentown Indians would be recruited by the British. The military intended to prevent any possibility of that from happening. As the militia escorted the Indians away from their homes several soldiers held back. They began to methodically ransack Greentown and then set it ablaze. Unfortunately for James Copus, the soldiers hadn't allowed sufficient time for the removal of the Indians before putting Greentown to the torch. The Indians could see smoke from the fires rising above the trees at their back and they rebelled. Fifty or more warriors broke away from their escort and quickly disappeared into the surrounding forest.

Marauding Indians, intent on revenge for the destruction of Greentown, attacked a number of isolated cabins, killing several white settlers. When The Reverend Copus got word of these attacks he understood quickly that he and his family were in danger. The Indians would assume that he had lied to them. Taking only enough time to gather a few small possessions, the family abandoned their log cabin and fled to a military blockhouse, one of many that had been hastily constructed across Richland County at the beginning of the war.

A few days later, assured by the military that the Indians had left the area and that the danger had passed, Copus and his family, accompanied by an escort of nine soldiers, returned to their home and were somewhat surprised to find it still standing and undamaged. The soldiers stayed the night. Early the next morning several of the soldiers, secure in the belief that the Indians had fled, left their guns at the cabin and walked to a nearby creek to get water. At the water's edge they were surprised by Indians who killed two of the unarmed men and chased the others into the woods. One man, wounded in the leg, managed to flee to the cabin. When Copus opened the door for the injured soldier the Reverend was struck in the chest by a musket ball fired by the pursuing Indians. Falling backward into the cabin he died a short time later. Barricading themselves inside, the surviving soldiers and the remaining Copus family awaited what they were sure was an imminent attack. It never came and by mid-day the Indians had left and never returned. The Greentown Indians, at least those not involved in the uprising, were eventually permitted to go to their relatives who had earlier joined with the Wyondots. All that remains of Greentown today is a roadside historical marker, although at this writing  a local historical group is attempting a reconstruction of the site.

I had come about as close to Helltown and to the native roots of the greater Malabar Farm area as I could hope to come. It was late and the gray ceiling overhead was darkening, a sure signal that it was time to turn for home. Compared to the hike in, the return trip was simple. To avoid retracing my steps across the mud flat I followed the Clearfork up stream for several hundred additional yards, the blue flashes of a kingfisher leading the way as it flitted from tree to tree along the river's edge, always keeping a few dozen yards ahead of me. I turned away from the river at a point where a deer trail cut through a wide expanse of knee-high scouring rushes. I had seen these rushes in sparse patches before, but never in such abundance. Scouring rushes are actually living fossils, being the only surviving member of a class of plants that flourished 100 million years ago. Also called horse tail and Dutch rush, their Latin name is *Equistum hyemale*, which translates as winter horse. The Lenape called the plant "laleniken," meaning scour grass. The name comes from the plant's rigid and hollow segmented stem with a fluted and raspy surface that feels like fine grit sandpaper. Found along waterways and in damp woodlands, this plant remains a pale green throughout the winter. It was used by both Indians and early settlers to clean pots and pans, thus the plant's popular name. Its scouring nature worked for me as well. Dragging my feet through these thick rushes removed much of the heavy gray mud that still clung so tenaciously to my boots.

If you have ever visited a natural history museum that displays the skeletons of giant dinosaurs then you will understand the vision that presented itself to me shortly after leaving the river and passing through the field of rushes. Rising before me, indistinct through the intervening trees, and contrasting sharply with the dark umber of the surrounding forest, was the gleaming sun bleached skeletal hulk of a stegosaurus, or possibly a triceratops, backbone arched as if frozen in mid-stride. At least that was my imaginative first impression upon seeing the large and barkless sycamore tree that lay nearly perpendicular across my path. The thick white trunk resembled a rigid spine; its middle branches the bent legs, smaller branches formed the rounded, though somewhat shattered, rib cage.

Standing alongside this slowly decaying giant I began to reflect upon my surroundings. I reluctantly came to the realization that what I was seeing was not what Captain Pipe and his Lenape companions would have seen. Yes, they would have observed many fallen trees, some of them brilliant white sycamore hulks like this one. In addition they would have witnessed how these trees, collapsing under their own weight, had slowly dissolved into the forest floor. However, they knew nothing of dinosaurs. They could never have compared a downed tree to some prehistoric behemoth. Pleasant Hill Reservoir, with its steely gray surface, was not part of the world they knew. The countless clusters of multi-flora rose that make hiking off trail so challenging today didn't exist on this continent when Indians ruled here. The gigantic oaks, black walnut, beech and white pine that the Indians would have known are mostly gone, replaced now by a second, third, and even fourth woodland that will likely never achieve the massive girth or height of the original forest's trees. The eastern forest of 21st century Richland County is only a shadow of what once was. The bear, the wolf, the rattlesnake, and the cougar are all gone. The land and the forest that was their home is now scored and fragmented by roads. The trees that today throw long finger-like shadows across my imaginary dinosaur, the trees that now grow throughout of the entirety of the eastern United States, are young. Their ancestors were cut down generations ago to make way for fields of corn and wheat, or to accommodate and fuel the unshackled industrial development, commercial growth, and population expansion of the past two centuries.[4]

As a preface to his 1933 autobiographical novel *The Farm*, Louis Bromfield wrote an open letter to his daughters. He had written the book to tell them something of the 19th century rural world of their grandfathers, a world that for his daughters had *"... become as remote as the tenth century."* In this novel Bromfield described his grandfather's world as something of an agricultural golden age, infinitely richer and more satisfying than the industrialized society that followed it. Perhaps Bromfield was being overly generous in his enthusiasm for those rustic bygone days; they had their own problems. However, the words he wrote for Anne, Hope, and Ellen still touch the heart. They could just as easily have been written about the wild land I had sought with my journey in search of Malabar Farm's native past.

> *"You may discover a stream or hill which you recognize from hearsay and legend, but that is all. The rest has vanished. One thing you would never find, and that is the feel of the country..."*

Some geographical features, the hills, the bluff along the river, the fundamental course of the river itself, the scouring rushes that fill the lowlands along the Clearfork's channel, these would have changed relatively little since Captain Pipe's days. These at least I could share with the Lenape chief. I could even listen to the same chatter of gray squirrels high overhead, and I could hear the same far off cries of crows. Still, in the end it wasn't quite enough. I was too conscious of the many things that have changed during the rush of the past two centuries. The echo of those past centuries quickly disappeared within the diminished forest that surrounded me, evaporating into the distant sound of an airplane overhead. Try as I might I could not hold the Lenape in sharp focus. As quickly as I drew forth a mental image of the Indians who once hunted and gathered in this place it slipped away like fog before the morning sun.

Perhaps that is why narratives such as those of Captain Pipe and the Lenape, stories of the virgin forest that was their home, tales of Helltown, Greentown, and of The Reverend James Copus, should not be forgotten. Such stories anchor us in place; they secure us within the greater currents of being and time. They enrich our days and add depth to our thoughts and dreams. They are a counter-weight to an arrogance that manifests itself in the greed of short term gain, an arrogance that recognizes only superficial gratification, an arrogance that, while often masquerading behind words of stewardship, reveals its true nature through actions that betray a profound disregard for the future sustainability of the earth and all of its inhabitants.

What dark tales might our descendants create to tell the story of our generations?

# Chapter 3

# Up Ferguson's Road

In 1944 Louis Bromfield published *The World We Live In,* a collection of short stories that had appeared earlier in Cosmopolitan magazine. Among the nine tales included in that volume was *"Up Ferguson Way"*. Critics of the day did not consider this story to be among the better pieces in the collection. One critic described it as of poor technical construction, with the author meandering too loosely while attempting to remain within the confines of the short story form. I disagree; I consider this story to be one of Louis Bromfield's most delightful and enchanting pieces of writing, revealing as much about the author's own personal inner landscape as it does his main character's world. Apparently, other people feel as I do. In 1981 the story was re-printed as its own illustrated sixty page book by The Tender Land Company of Mansfield, Ohio, and the story was recently re-issued in a new edition by the Wooster Book Company. A word of caution pertaining to this short story is needed here. In Louis Bromfield's first non-fiction book *Pleasant Valley* (1945) he included a chapter titled "Up Ferguson Way." This is not the same story as the one in his 1944 collection. The 1944 short story "Up Ferguson Way," though primarily a work of fiction, does, however, incorporate real people and real locations in its telling. Bromfield even inserted himself into the story as a character/narrator. He did this so convincingly that many people today believe the story to be a true, if somewhat fanciful tale.

The fictional *"Up Ferguson Way"* is the story of Zenobia Ferguson, a young woman living alone on the isolated farmstead that has been left to her by her father. Late one night she accidentally shoots and kills her lover, having mistaken him for a bandit. Zenobia lives out the remainder of her long life alone on the remote hilltop farm, her only companions being the wild animals with which she shares a mystical bond.

The character of Zenobia Ferguson was based on a real person, Phoebe Wise, a distant relative of Louis Bromfield. Phoebe, born sometime around 1850 in Mansfield, Ohio, was an eccentric individual. She inherited a small farm on the outskirts of town and resided there alone. Though considered attractive and quite intelligent by all who knew her, Phoebe remained in body and spirit closer to the animals, both tame and wild, that shared her farm than to the citizens of Mansfield. In spite of, or perhaps because of, her peculiar ways, the citizens of Mansfield retained an abiding affection for their strange neighbor. As a young woman Phoebe Wise found herself the target of a stalker named Jacob Kastanowitz, who repeatedly threatened to kidnap her and carry her south to be married. Restraining orders issued by the court failed to stop this harassment and late one night Phoebe's stalker attempted to force his way into her house through the kitchen door. After warning him that she had a gun, Phoebe fired a rifle shot through the door and all went quiet. The next morning Kastanowitz's dead body was found on the ground near the porch. Following a brief investigation the shooting was declared justified. Phoebe went on to live a long life, dying on March 13, 1933. Phoebe Wise, whom Louis Bromfield had known as a young man, would become the inspiration for characters in several of his short stories and novels.

While the true story of Phoebe Wise took place on the far northeastern edge of Mansfield, decades before and more than twenty miles north of Malabar Farm, Bromfield chose to place the homestead of his fictional Zenobia Ferguson within the boundaries of his farm, thus weaving his tale into the local history of his own land. Even today at Malabar Farm State Park there is a Ferguson Meadow high on the most remote part of the farm. The way up to the meadow follows the remnants of an old dirt lane, known in the nineteenth century as the Ferguson Road or Newville Road. This road once took travelers past the doorstep of the Ferguson homestead and beyond that an additional two miles to the small town of Newville. The namesake of this old road and of today's farm meadow was not, however, the Ferguson found in Bromfield's story. Bromfield borrowed the locale of the distant meadow hilltop, along with the last name of an early Richland County pioneer, for use in his fictional tale.

William Ferguson, for whom both the Ferguson Road and Ferguson Meadow were named, was an early settler in Pleasant Valley, having come from Pennsylvania in the first decade of the 19th century. He lived high on the hill that now defines the southern boundaries of Malabar Farm. In the mid-nineteenth century the Ferguson/Newville Road, an important route for farm products leaving the eastern end of Pleasant Valley, passed only yards in front of the Ferguson home. A short section of that old dirt road still survives as the lane that takes Park visitors to the Malabar Farm Sugar Shack and Pugh Cabin. The majority of the Ferguson Road has, however, been abandoned. Although most of it has been neglected for perhaps a hundred years now, this ancient wagon route had an important role to play in the creation of this book. Its surviving end, that part that currently links Bromfield Road to Malabar's Sugar Shack, would be the starting point for four out of the five hikes described here.

For some time I had considered the idea of following the old Ferguson Road as far as it would take me, hopefully all the way to Newville. Finally on an early March morning I decided to act on that idea. My walk began where the lane leading to today's Malabar Farm Sugar Shack meets with Bromfield Road. The old road had been built during the first half of the nineteenth century, probably before 1835. Prior to that time the early "roads" leaving Pleasant Valley were not much more than dirt paths, sometimes following old Indian trails. For the most part they were suitable only for travel by foot or on horseback. As populations grew these foot paths were widened to allow for wagon use, although they were frequently rendered impassable during periods of heavy rain, when they quickly became muddy quagmires. At the time of its construction the Ferguson Road became the most direct route to Newville for farmers living in lower end of Pleasant Valley.

A hundred and fifty years ago, as lightning bolts split the sky and violent summer storms sent sheets of rain cascading down hillsides, dirt roads, their surfaces cut and loosened by countless horses hooves, could quickly become broad streams of frothy brown water. When the rains finally ended, these roads were often left a muddy and eroded mess, rendered temporarily impassable for anything on wheels. Even travel by foot or on horseback might result in an unintended adventure. It was the periodic grading of such roads, necessary to restore them to functional use after repeated cloud bursts, which left many country roads deeply sunken below the level of the surrounding countryside. Thunderstorm damage would be especially acute where a dirt road crossed a steep hill, as the Ferguson Road did in a place that a century later would be called Malabar Farm.

Much of the still functional Malabar portion of the old Ferguson Road passes beneath a tunnel of trees, its bed cut deeply into the hillside of the bordering forest. Even today heavy rains occasionally overflow shallow ditches, methodically eating away at the edges of the road's hard packed surface. Beyond the Sugar Shack there is a much rougher section of the road that remains passable to Ferguson Meadow. There are places here where the roadbed runs four or five feet below the forest floor. On the far side of the meadow, Ferguson Road has been completely abandoned for generations, surviving only as a sunken and overgrown remnant, a tree filled depression, a reminder not only of man's ability to modify his landscape, but also of nature's ability to fight back, to reclaim its own.

The great hulk of an ancient beech tree stands guard over the entrance to the Ferguson/Newville Road. Its top was broken off ages ago; what remains is ragged and weather beaten. The gray trunk, much of its bark slowly peeling away, is pocked by countless blackened woodpecker holes. The few branches that somehow remain are gnarled and broken. Against all odds one branch still struggles to put forth a few green leaves each spring. It is likely that a hundred and fifty years ago, horse drawn farm wagons, creaking under the weight of their heavy loads, passed within the shade of this beech's outstretched limbs as they made their way up the road to Newville. Approaching this enduring

Old Friends.

giant always brings to mind one of my favorite works of art, Winslow Homer's watercolor painting *"Old Friends."* The subject of this painting is a bearded and aging Adirondack mountain guide. His woolen shirt, sleeves rolled up to the elbow, is tucked

73

into baggy canvas trousers that are held up with braces. The old man is standing alongside the broken and barkless trunk of a once great tree, his arm reaches out to gently press a palm against the tree's now lifeless form. Although a walk along Malabar's maintained section of the old lane is an enjoyable stroll at any time of the year, I chose this bright early March morning for my exploration of Ferguson's Road. It was sugar maple time at Malabar and the sugar maple trees lining the road were hungwith buckets collecting sap. The process of collecting and making maple syrup is a fascinating activity. Maple sap flows best when nighttime temperatures fall below freezing but the days are above 32 degrees. The sugar content in the sap of sugar maple trees, while higher than that of other trees, still averages only about 2 %. It takes from forty to fifty gallons of sap to produce a

single gallon of syrup. Even with modern collecting equipment and efficient evaporators this makes for a very labor intensive operation.

Native Americans knew how to make maple syrup, though exactly how they first discovered this time consuming activity remains a mystery. A wooden bowl or a carved-out log would be filled with maple sap and red hot rocks dropped into the watery liquid. The hot rocks would slowly boil the water away, leaving the Indians with a sweet but somewhat messy syrup, contaminated as it often was with bits of leaves, tiny flecks of stone, and small fragments of wood. Before Europeans introduced honeybees onto the North American continent, maple syrup was the Indian's only sweetener. Early settlers improved on the syrup making process by boiling their sap in a series of large iron kettles that were suspended over wood fires. The resulting hot syrup would be poured into a wooden trough, where it was worked back and forth with a wooden paddle for fifteen to twenty minutes. When exposed to the air the hot syrup would gradually cool and crystallize, becoming maple sugar. Before refrigeration it was difficult to store maple syrup for any length of time, and it was nearly impossible to transport it any great distance. Maple sugar, however, could be put into sacks, making it easy to both store and transport. Because it was a much more practical product, maple sugar quickly became the typical end result of maple syrup season. Now you know why the buildings that shelter today's modern maple sap evaporators are called "sugar shacks" and not "syrup shacks."

From late spring through early October the overarching branches of tall trees form a high green canopy that cools the Ferguson roadbed. On hot August days the air beneath this cover can be ten to twelve degrees lower than that in nearby open fields. However, on this late winter morning the leafless trees remained dormant, their buds only hinting of spring. The open woodland, devoid of leaf, was a bird watchers delight. I am, I have to admit, a dullard when it comes to identifying more than a few birds. I know the blue jay, the cardinal, the American crow, red-tail hawk, and the barred owl. I can recognize chickadees, sparrows, nuthatches, the titmouse, and the gold finch. Recently I learned what a towhee looks like. Still, I am at a total loss when it comes to identifying all but a very few bird songs.[5]

Fortunately there was no mistaking the bald eagle that this early March morning revealed itself to me as it passed overhead, just beyond the uppermost branches of the tallest trees. The bird's massive wings beat a slow and graceful rhythm as it crossed the fields and pastures of Malabar, headed in the general direction of The Clearfork River and Pleasant Hill Reservoir, only a mile or two north and east of Malabar Farm. The bird's ample body, with its great white head and its large hooked beak, left no doubt as to identification. Bald Eagles have only recently returned to this area. They are most often observed at the reservoir and along the Clearfork River. This eagle sighting was an event in itself, but it was only the first of two delightful birding experiences I was to enjoy on this walk. No sooner had the eagle passed beyond my sight than a clamorous squawking erupted in the woods to my right. There, no more than fifty feet away and exuberantly flitting from tree to tree, was a pair of pileated woodpeckers. I have seen these largest of the woodpeckers previously while on hikes at Malabar but not often. They usually prefer the seclusion of deep woods, and to find them here along the lower reaches of Ferguson's Road was a delight. This wary couple, hopefully a mating pair, moved so quickly from trunk to trunk and branch to branch that I found it impossible to get a photograph of them.

The pileated woodpecker, with its black body and black and white head crowned by a prominent red crest, was the inspiration for Walter Lantz's mischievous cartoon character Woody the Woodpecker, but I will reserve the telling of that story for a later chapter. Where automobile travel ends at a point about a half mile up Ferguson lane there is a small parking area, two log cabins, and Malabar Farm's Sugar Shack. Beyond the Sugar Shack the old Ferguson Road narrows, becoming deeper and much rougher. This sunken lane remains passable up to Ferguson Meadow and hiking is encouraged, but automobiles are prohibited. Two small ponds add to the rustic atmosphere of the log cabins. These ponds were built by James Pugh shortly after he constructed the log cabins in 1938 and 1956. Louis Bromfield would also construct several ponds on his own property when he established Malabar Farm. His and Pugh's purpose in creating these ponds was manifold. They wanted to insure a supply of water in times of drought. They also placed the ponds near important buildings in case of fire. When completed the ponds were stocked with fish as a source of both recreation and food. It wasn't long before turtles, frogs, wild ducks, geese, egrets, and even a muskrat or two were also taking advantage of the water. Both Bromfield and Pugh had a love of all animals, domestic and wild. I am sure that they had the needs of wild nature in mind when they created their ponds. Wild nature, while not his primary subject, was not neglected in Louis Bromfield's writing.

The last book that Louis Bromfield published was a non-fiction collection of stories titled *Animals and Other People* (1955). In this book Bromfield brought together many of his best and most popular stories about animals and the people that he thought of as "teched." The teched were those rare individuals who enjoyed a special kinship with animals. In this volume the reader will find stories about the dogs of Malabar, especially the boxers so loved by the author. Also included are stories about a Guernsey bull named Sylvester; Mummy, a big female tiger cat; Thomas, an irascible parrot; and Gilbert, a wild tom turkey. Bromfield also wrote of seeing wild rabbits frolicking in the moonlight of a snow covered winter evening. He told of hearing the barking of foxes sitting high on the sandstone cliffs behind the Big House, and of seeing them silhouetted against the fire of a summer sunset. He told of seeing the black tip of a nose and the expanding V wake that spread out behind a muskrat as it swam across the pond below his Big House. Among the teched people that he wrote about were the eccentric Phoebe Wise, Johnny

Appleseed, and the unnamed (fictional?) farmer featured in *"My Ninety Acres."* Bromfield also wrote of his great-aunt Mattie, who loved to quote from Samuel Taylor Coleridge's "The Rime of the Ancient Mariner"

*He prayeth well, who loveth well*
*Both man and bird and beast.*

*He prayeth best, who loveth best*
*All things both great and small*

*For the dear God who loveth us,*
*He made and loveth all.*

Aunt Mattie, aged, and blind since the age of thirty, still loved to be taken out into the fields and pastures to sit by a rippling stream where she could feel the breeze on her face, listen to the cattle lowing, and hear the birds singing in the trees. The poem that she loved to recite also spoke to the heart of her great-nephew, for Louis Bromfield can surely be counted among the teched.

Beyond the Sugar Shack the old road begins a final serpentine assent of the hill. Here the route grows steeper before finally leveling off at Ferguson Meadow. For most of this route the lane is deeply sunken. In the aftermath of a season of snow and rain, the way can be quite muddy, despite the tons of stone that have been heaped upon it over the years. In the summer this upper lane continues as a green tunnel with wild and ragged grape vines dangling overhead and the forest crowding in along its high banks. In March, however, only the evergreen of Christmas ferns interrupts the dull gray and brown of the surrounding woods. The lane widens at a point about half way up to the meadow, taking a gently arcing turn away from the original Ferguson route. For about a hundred yards this "new" road runs parallel to the original, before joining it again. The abandoned portion of original road, though straight and deep, is barely recognizable, being filled now with scraggly trees, wild and weedy brush, and thick clusters of thorny multi-flora rose. I don't know when or why this by-pass was constructed. This area of the Ohio countryside is well known for its abundance of natural springs. In *Pleasant Valley* Louis Bromfield wrote of cleaning and reopening more than twenty springs at Malabar Farm. Perhaps this abandoned stretch of Ferguson's Road was located near one of those springs and being chronically wet had become too difficult to maintain.

From where the lane resumes its original route it follows a curving line of several hundred yards to the top of the hill and the Ferguson Meadow. This portion of the original road is also deeply sunken. Winds, blowing through the high open stretches of the nearby hilltop meadow, often leave this part of the road strewn with broken branches, and today was no exception. I took a little time to do some "trail maintenance" before I continued my climb. This activity got me to thinking. The debris I was clearing from the trail today was the result of natural forces; wind, rain, ice, and age. What is it about some people that they can so casually toss

The old road to Newville.

aside their empty plastic bottles, candy wrappers, and aluminum cans? What makes them different from those of us who make a habit of carrying bags along on hikes so that we can pick up their trash? What do people who so thoughtlessly dispose of their scraps take away from a walk in these woods? When I see what they have left behind I wonder why these individuals even made the effort to come here. What was it that they were looking for on their walk? It is bad enough to see litter on the trail itself, but I sometimes find plastic bottles that have been thrown some distance into the surrounding woods. Worse yet, I have found trash deliberately tossed into locations that make it dangerous or even impossible to retrieve them. Such questions are not new, and I have no answers for them. It doesn't matter how many candy wrappers I pick up, I still wonder... why here, why anywhere?

Although I took this walk on a cool March day, Ferguson's Meadow is one of my favorite destinations on warm summer afternoons. Spreading out in a general east to west direction, approximately a half mile long and 200 yards wide, the meadow is bisected by the remnants of the Old Ferguson Road. The smaller portion of the meadow lies to the west of that road. Here the encircling forest seems to be slowly closing in. Edges are now ragged with pines and other succession species that are slowly intruding into the open spaces of the field. Although farm workers do occasionally cut the grass here, clusters of small trees and shrubs have taken hold within the open grassy spaces, and now form little "islands" throughout the expanse of the clearing. This section of the meadow reminds me of photographs I have seen of Japanese Zen gardens, although here the raked gravel encircling stone islands has been replaced with windblown grass skirting tree clusters. This western side of Ferguson's Meadow, being somewhat wilder than the section to the east of the road is, in late summer, home to a large array of purple crowned thistles and the multitude of butterflies and bumblebees that swarm over them.

The eastern and larger side of the meadow is, for the most

part, an open expanse of coarse grasses. Here the farm staff has until recently continued to cut hay. I believe that this haying was recently terminated because of the remoteness of the meadow and the relatively poor quality of the grasses. When the cutting and baling was still being done the flat plane of the meadow would be broken with picturesque bales of tightly rolled grass, the shredded wheat bales so familiar to summer motorists along many country roads. On the eastern meadow, near the old lane, several very old apple trees stand. In the spring their pink blossoms provide a delightful accent to the mass of spring green that dominates the view in every direction except up. When Louis Bromfield purchased this property in 1939 he wrote that you could see into several surrounding counties from the clearing atop Ferguson Meadow. Since that time the trees encircling this field have had more than seventy years to grow, creating a living wall of green and brown that now precludes such a view. Mixed among the hardwoods and pines that border the northern edges of the meadow are the aged survivors of an old apple orchard. In early autumn gnarled branches still hang heavy with clusters of small red apples streaked with yellow. Several years ago my wife and I collected a bag of these apples and a few days later we enjoyed homemade Malabar apple pies.

Toward the far end of the meadow there is a stand of several hundred sugar maples planted in rows in the mid-1970s, shortly after Malabar Farm became State property. These trees, some now approaching a tapping diameter of about fourteen inches, are special "super maples." They are hybrids, and are expected to produce a sap with three to four percent sugar, twice the sugar content of natural sugar maples. They ended up in this high distant meadow because at the time they were developed there was little interest expressed in cultivating them. It was on the low grasses growing among these rows of super maples that during a mid-August afternoon my wife and I had spread a blanket and were enjoying a simple picnic when we discovered that we had caught the attention of an inquisitive doe. Standing statue like not more than thirty feet away, her tawny coat merged almost seamlessly with the browning grasses that hid her legs, providing a near perfect camouflage that rendered the animal almost invisible. For several minutes we watched the doe watching us. The surrounding sunlit green of maple leaves glinted sharply in her brown eyes. Then, apparently satisfied that we meant her no harm, she casually grazed her way into the darker shadows of the surrounding woods, where she disappeared.

As far as any practical travel is concerned where I emerged onto the open meadow marks the end of Ferguson Road. Beyond the meadow the lane has been abandoned for generations. Where it had once crossed the flat of the meadow all evidence of the road has been erased. On the far side of the meadow the remnant of the roadbed reappears, but is slowly being reabsorbed into the surrounding forest. The road's narrow, low banked depression is now choked with weeds, small trees, wild roses and even wilder looking grape vines. Unless one is familiar with the early history of Pleasant Valley and Newville it is unlikely that this depression in the landscape would be recognized as once having been a busy highway. It was here, descending the far side of the hill, that a Columbia Gas pipeline was laid parallel to the abandoned road. The Columbia Gas-Weaver Operations is located less than a mile from Malabar Farm and natural gas rights-of-way cross the Park in several places. There are also two natural gas wells on Park property. They were here long before Louis Bromfield ever dreamed of Malabar Farm. The original lease agreements for these wells date back to 1910.

The bridle and hiking trail that circles Malabar Farm emerges from the woods to the west of Ferguson Meadow. This trail bisects the western meadow until it reaches the old road, then turns south to briefly follow the gas line downhill and away from the meadow. The trail doesn't remain on the gas line for long before it veers to the east, where it follows its own course through the wooded hillside roughly parallel to the meadow. The sunken and vegetation choked old roadbed, running in line with the

Columbia Gas right-of way, continues in a straight line down the hill. The gas line provided me with a convenient open path to follow along the abandoned road's eastern flank.

As I followed the gas line downhill, the Ferguson Road, its sunken bed choked with trees and underbrush, remained visible on my right. At a slight leveling of the ground several hundred feet beyond the bridle trail there is a faint path, barely visible beneath the heavy leaf cover that blankets the forest floor. It angles to the right and toward the old lane. Turning onto this narrow path I cautiously stepped over a tangle of rusted barbed wire that had formerly bordered the old road. Once clear of the grasping snags of the wire, I edged down the sloping embankment and into the old roadbed. With its sides slowly collapsing inward the road is now no more than a dozen feet wide. Scrambling up the opposite bank and over more wire placed me in the general locale of a spot identified on Malabar Farm hiking maps as either "The Ferguson Homestead," or "The Ferguson Steps." It was a hundred and fifty years ago on this tree covered hillside that William Ferguson, namesake of Ferguson Road and Ferguson Meadow, replaced his log cabin home with a small two story frame house. William had worked hard to clear the land surrounding his home, now it is once again heavily wooded.

The Ferguson homestead, c.1890    photograph courtesy Malabar Farm State Park.

The Ferguson homestead today.

     Unfortunately William Ferguson's frame house burned down in the early years of the 20th century, and it takes a little investigation to locate where it once stood. All that remains now are a few scattered chimney bricks, the concrete steps that once stood before the front porch, and a shallow cellar hole, its depression identifiable as man-made by some hand cut stone slabs that roughly define a portion of its perimeter. The concrete steps, three high, present a singularly haunting sight, surrounded as they are by the wild nature that has slowly and methodically obliterated nearly all other evidence of human occupation. Seeing these steps, in this environment, brought to mind a late afternoon photograph that I had taken years ago. The subject was a cracked and weathered concrete sidewalk slab. Reaching upward through one especially wide crack were the dark green leaves of a dandelion. From the center of these leaves grew a thin translucent stem. The stem drooped slightly from the weight of a bright yellow flower that crowned it. The stem and the flower cast a long dark shadow across the roughened surface of the cement. In his first farm book *Pleasant Valley* (1945) Louis Bromfield wrote that, although the Ferguson house had burned down long before his arrival, two ancient Norway spruces that had once graced the front yard still stood tall. Even those remnants of the Ferguson years have disappeared. Change comes more quickly to living things than it does to concrete, brick, and stone.

Born in Pennsylvania in 1776, William Ferguson was among the earliest white men to enter the land that would one day become Malabar Farm. In 1802, the year before Ohio became a State, he purchased land near Steubenville in Jefferson County. By 1805 he was in what would soon become Richland County, seeking to trade for furs with the Lenape Indians who were living in this area at the time. Upon his arrival here he built a log cabin on a level shelf of a hillside, just below the summit of a high, heavily wooded ridge. This cabin served as his headquarters as he traveled the region searching for Indians and the furs they might wish to trade. Over the next few years William Ferguson made several trips to this area, living in his cabin while he continued his trading.

The trade in furs that attracted William Ferguson to the wilds of Ohio was a primary influence on the opening of the North American continent. It also had a long range negative impact on the Indians, who quickly became dependent on a long list of goods that European traders offered for their furs. Among the trade goods that the Indians desired but could not manufacture for themselves were iron axes, hatchets, knives, awls, fish hooks, cloth, wool blankets, brass kettles, muskets, lead, and gun powder. It wasn't long before the fur traders had also introduced whiskey into Indian society. Eager to secure such goods the Indians traded for them with beaver, otter, mink, fox, bear, and deer skins. The most important of these by far were the beaver pelts. Competition for the best hunting grounds intensified among the various Indian tribes following the arrival of the Europeans with their ever increasing demand for furs.

Tensions among the Europeans themselves exacerbated the problem for the Indians, as the English,the French, and the Dutch all sought to control the fur trade and to dominate of the North American continent in general. The Indians knew that they were being manipulated, but they also knew that they were now dependent on trade goods. Against their own long-term best interests they found themselves hopelessly entangled in the European intrigues that ultimately came to a head with the French and Indian War of the 1750s. Although that war was eventually decided in favor of the British, it was only three decades later that the American Revolutionary War would force the British to move north to Canada. The new American Government took control of the fur trade within its borders, a trade that by the early years of the nineteenth century was already an industry in decline. Fashions had changed; beaver was no longer in demand, and many Indian tribes were finding it increasingly difficult to locate the fur bearing animals that the surviving trade depended on. This scarcity of animals was especially severe east of the Mississippi River. The fur trade that did continue moved to the frontiers of the American West, but by the 1830's even that had collapsed.

William Ferguson had come into the business at the tail-end of the fur trade in the East, and probably found the work less lucrative than he had hoped. In any event he found the Ohio country to his liking and in 1815 moved his entire family to the Ohio wilderness, settling them on the hillside where he had a decade earlier built his fur trading cabin. He began clearing land and soon had established a small farm. At first the family lived in the log cabin; sometime later they built the frame home shown in the photo. The old cabin was then turned into a barn.[6]

Over the years Ferguson made improvements to his farm, clearing more land and planting an orchard. As he grew older his son John took over operations on the farm, officially purchasing the land in 1847. William Ferguson died in 1851. He, his wife Jane, his father-in-law, and three grandchildren are buried in the

Olivet Cemetery on Malabar Farm. John Ferguson sold the farm to his son Isaac in 1891 and died that same year. John Ferguson was buried in the Pleasant Valley Lutheran Cemetery near Malabar Farm. When Louis Bromfield purchased the Clem Herring farm in 1939 the deed to that property included the hilltop acreage still being referred to as the old Ferguson Place, although Herring had purchased the property from Isaac Ferguson in 1922.

I continued my walk beyond the Ferguson homestead by following the pipeline rather than trying to walk in the old roadbed, as that route is obstructed in many places by fallen trees and thickets of thorny multi-flora rose. After passing over the high meadow the old Ferguson Road descends into a valley before once again rising on its final ascent up and out of Pleasant Valley. A narrow and slow moving creek flows through the notch of this valley. The stream's unhurried path cuts across both pipeline and roadbed, the shallow trickle of water passing almost unnoticed beneath one's feet. The tiny run even disappears in places where it wanders beneath tight clumps of weeds and the high arcing grasses that bracket it. I knew from past experience, however, that there was more to this middling little trace of water than first meets the eye.

Turning to my left and away from the pipeline I followed the weaving path of the creek several hundred yards downstream to where it enters a low channel of hard sandstone. Slowly gathering speed as it flows along this smooth and unobstructed path, the tiny stream suddenly disappears over a rocky shelf. Standing on cliff's edge, I looked down into a deep and winding ravine, its steep sides stitched together with an expanse of widely spaced trees and the gray-green faces of numerous moss covered sandstone outcroppings. The little stream continued on its slow and relentless way far below me. From my vantage point high above, the water appeared as a slender thread of sparkling silver, weaving its way through a tumbled bed of rock and rounded boulders. Surely it has taken many thousands of years for such a leisurely flow of water to have carved out this dramatic and beautiful vale. I have visited this place before and on each occasion it has inspired a certain hushed awe.

Ferguson Falls is the rather grand name given the middling cliff top plunge of this unnamed little rivulet. With the exception of a few weeks in springtime and during occasions of heavy rain in other seasons, the little brook that runs over the sandstone ledge doesn't produce much of a falls. It isn't the falls, however, that makes this place special. Climbing cautiously down and into the ravine I edged my way slowly along its rocky wall until I came to a deeply recessed hollow, hidden beneath a massive horizontal slab of gray-green stone. Melting curtains of winter ice still draped the grainy surfaces of surrounding stones. The dense sedimentary formations that bracket this monolithic block are clothed year round in green mosses and overhung with grasses and Christmas ferns. The block itself is bare save for a splotchy patina of pale green lichen. This table-like slab of stone spans much of the ravine.

Its upper surface forms the shelf over which the little creek tumbles.   A shallow cave lays hidden behind the shimmering curtain of the falling water. Visible in the shadowy recesses of the cave are crumbling layers of brown and yellow sedimentary sandstone, millions of years in the making. This sandstone, formed on the deltas of a primeval sea, provided the raw material for the natural sculpting by the stream that followed. Although the walls of the cave are damp in places, its floor is covered with dry, coarsely textured sand. Louis Bromfield once

Ferguson Falls

wrote of finding Indian artifacts here. Looking into the ravine and the surrounding forest I could imagine this small cave having been a place of shelter for early woodland Indians, people who found refuge here long before either the Lenape or William Ferguson laid claim to it.

Ferguson Falls is one of the more remote and thus wilder locations at Malabar Farm. Here, surviving along the steep sides of the deep ravine, are oak, hickory, beech and maple trees older and of greater height than most anywhere else on the farm. They thrive in this place because the steep sides of the ravine made logging these trees too difficult to be cost effective. Here, at Ferguson's Falls, the forest looks ancient, here it looks as it must have looked when William Ferguson first came to this land in search of Indians to trade with.

Retracing my steps to where the little stream trickled across the gas line brought me back to the furthest point that I had ever walked on this side of Malabar Farm. What lay beyond this nameless brook was something of a mystery. Ferguson Road can be found on an 1877 plat map for Richland County, and the road had a significant part to play in the 1896 true-crime story of Ceely Rose, a tale that that I will return to in Chapter Six. Thus, as late as the end of the 19th century a traveler would have been able to follow the road all the way from Pleasant Valley to the town of Newville. At that time the entire length of the road crossed private land, a major portion of its route still does. However, I did not know how much of the road remained, whether I would recognize it, and whether I would be able to follow it to Newville.

Beyond the notch of the valley, with its narrow run that struggles to be a stream, the old road and the pipeline pursue a direct course straight up hill. I would have found the going here very difficult had it not been for the gas company right-of-away. The hillside is covered with thick, broad clusters of multi-flora rose. In spots even the edges of the pipeline are crowded by this wild rose. Its thorny stems and branches reach in from the sides to snag pant leg and sleeve. Multi-flora rose, so abundant and so problematic in this area, is an invasive species that was foolishly presented to farmers decades ago as a natural alternative to fencing. The plant, a thorny shrub from Asia, was first introduced into the United States in 1866 as an ornamental. In the 1930s the U.S. Conservation Service, along with various State Conservation Departments encouraged its use by land owners as a "living fence." It was also promoted as an excellent cover for all variety of small game animals, from cottontail rabbits to quail. According to these experts, multi-flora rose also had the additional benefit of being an excellent source of food for song birds. This plant was widely and vigorously promoted as a benefit for both man and beast.

Louis Bromfield was approached by state conservation personnel, and being familiar with hedgerows of Europe, became convinced of the rose's value. He used his fame and his gift for communication to promote its use. He also practiced what he preached, planting multi-flora rose "fences" widely across Malabar Farm. In the spring the rose's sweet smelling white flowers still decorate the rural countryside, but now multi-flora rose is classified as an undesirable, and Bromfield gets much of the blame for its aggressive advance across the southern Richland County landscape. The blame should not be his exclusively or even primarily. Bromfield was, like most other farmers, taken in by the glowing words of experts. The blot on his reputation comes from his enthusiastic willingness to use his name and his writing skills to promote the plant much more effectively than would have otherwise been possible.

The unforeseen problem with multi-flora rose is the manner in which it spreads. A single plant can produce a half a million or more seeds each year. During the summer the white flowers develop into red fruits called hips. The hips, filled with seeds, cling to the plant year round, birds feed on them, then deposit the seeds in their droppings wherever they choose to fly. In the event these seeds don't immediately find suitable conditions to germinate they can remain viable in the soil for decades. As if this wasn't an adequate enough method for dispersal and survival, the arching stems of multi-flora rose can take root where they bend to touch the ground. They can literally "walk" across the countryside, often producing nearly impenetrable masses of thorn covered vegetation as they go.

As it spreads multi-flora rose monopolizes sunlight, moisture, and soil nutrients, to the serious disadvantage of native plants. The plant also causes farmers much grief as it rapidly creeps into pastures and diminishes forage.[7] My own family has its story to tell about this alien species. In the late 1950s my grandfather, with the encouragement of those who should have known better, planted multi-flora rose along the front of his Pennsylvania farmhouse, where it was to serve as a barrier to the dusty dirt road that passed so near his front porch. The roses spread rapidly and were soon growing unchecked in the fence rows of his fields and pastures. From there the plant began invading the fields themselves. Years later it took uncounted of hours of digging to remove the original roses from near the house, where they were threatening to take over the entire yard. Today multi-flora rose continues to grow wild elsewhere across the farm, requiring periodic brush-hogging to keep the borders of fields free of this unwanted guest, invited though it once was. A tree lined lane that divides fields for nearly the length of my grandfather's property is now impassable. Once a wonderful place to stroll, it is now choked shut in most places by the intertwining stems and painful snags of multi-flora rose.

As I climbed the Columbia Gas Line beyond the tiny brook, thick clusters of the thorny plant encroached in many places. Spiky stems reached out to snag any piece of cloth that came within their range. One finger was painfully bloodied when I tried to disengage my coat from a particularly unfriendly thorn. I found myself offering a sarcastic "Thank you, Mr. Bromfield!" to the surrounding forest and the gray sky overhead. Fortunately most of the rose bushes are being held at bay, at least for the time being, by the somewhat compacted soil of the gas-line. Near the crest of the ridge the rose bushes begin to thin out. There are places here where the rose's relative absence makes it feasible to leave the gas-line, cross over to the old roadbed, and actually walk in it for some distance. In doing so, the evidence of Mother Nature's ongoing work of reclamation becomes very evident. The road's high sides are slowly collapsing inward, and its floor is covered in many places with black pools of stagnant leaf filled water. Fallen trees, looking like gnarled toll gates, lay scattered across the roadbed at every imaginable angle. Living trees grow in great profusion throughout the lane's length, making it impossible to walk in a straight line for any distance. Several times I was forced to leave the road temporarily and circle around obstructions.

Standing in the middle of the lane, I closed my eyes and

imagined myself standing on this very spot in the mid-nineteenth century. I could see the tree lined road extending before me in a straight line to the open top of the hill. From there it seemed to launch itself into a blue and cloud dappled sky. Behind me I could hear the creaking approach of a wagon. Turning to look I could see that the wagon was heavy with the bountiful produce of surrounding fields. It would be necessary to step aside, to press myself against the high bank as the groaning wagon passed. In my mind's eye I could imagine the wagon being pulled by a team of straining horses, their heads down, massive muscles bulging. As the team lumbered past me the peculiar and pungent odor of dust mixed with horse sweat filled my nostrils. I could see the deep clefts being cut into the loose dirt by the horses' hoofs and the compressed ruts that were formed by the iron rimmed wheels of the wagon. A short distance behind the wagon came a noisy flock of unruly white geese, hurried on by their elderly and somewhat vexed master. I could see his straw hat tipped low over his

Walking in the old Newville Road.

93

forehead, its tattered rim hiding his aging eyes. From his sweat stained cotton shirtsleeve extended a muscled and darkly tanned arm. In his clenched fist he held a long, curved staff that he swung in broad arcs toward the tail feathers of his recalcitrant birds. Opening my eyes, this vision quickly evaporated, disappearing in the clear mid-day light and the dozens of trees that clogged the lane all around me. How many more decades would pass before this abandoned stretch of Ferguson's Road disappeared so completely that only the most dedicated and observant individual would be able to read the landscape and detect its route, or even its very existence?

Continuing my walk I noted that a drab gray sky had begun show through the trees at the horizon line of the ridge, suggesting that an opening lay just beyond the crest. About a hundred yards short of the hilltop I became aware of what appeared to be a half dozen large, watermelon shaped and randomly scattered black stones laying across the far path. Why had I not noticed these stones earlier? As I approached them the black stones erupted in a startled flurry of wings and feathers that quickly disappeared into the surrounding underbrush. There was a time in the recent past when wild turkeys were nearly extinct in this area. Now they have returned in large numbers, and are frequently seen foraging in fields and along roadsides of Pleasant Valley.

Moving forward I soon crested the hill, and both gas line and old road passed beyond the dark cover of surrounding forest to emerge into open air. Spreading out below me, the gray and unobstructed sky illuminating it like a theater stage, was a grass covered field. The field extended  downward to a distant and wooded edge. From that edge the landscape appeared to drop off in a steep and forested decline. At my immediate front grew a narrow width of wild, tangled, and tree choked vegetation that extended in a straight line down the middle of the field. I could imagine that the forest had slowly reclaimed other nearby fields, leaving only this one extant, mute testimony to earlier days, days when William Ferguson and the farmers of Pleasant Valley had cleared the land and hauled the products of their labor to markets in Newville.

The "narrow width of wild, tangled, and tree choked vegetation" is all that remains of the old Ferguson Road as it cuts a straight path through the middle of the field. A hundred and fifty yards long and perhaps a dozen feet wide, it is dense with a profusion of tall weeds, sumac, and the tightly interwoven stems of multi-flora rose. Mixed in this chaotic growth are broad thickets of low and scraggly trees. So thick is the vegetation here that I could barely see through it to the section of field that lay on its far side. What had once been a road now appears impenetrable by anything larger than a rabbit or a quail. In studying this portion of the old road the impression that I had was one of looking at a long, thin island of wilderness. This was a rather ironic notion, considering that historically, the roads opened the wild frontier to civilization. Here the road itself had become the wilderness, surrounded and circumscribed by a domesticated grassland.

The wavering outer edge of this dense growth was fringed in the over-arcing branches of staghorn sumac (genus *rhus),* their drooping ends heavy with tightly clustered reddish brown fruits. These fruits, called drupes, stood out in silhouette against the somber sky, looking like so many long forgotten Christmas ornaments. This fruit of the staghorn sumac can be used to make a beverage variously called, sumacade, rhus juice, and Indian lemonade. The stems of staghorn sumac have a soft pith core, making the plant a favorite of traditional Indian pipe makers. Indians once used staghorn leaves and fruit, combined with tobacco, to make smoking mixtures. Be warned, however, that you are certain of the plant's identity should you ever consider making a sumac beverage. Some forms of sumac are highly toxic. Poison sumac can be identified by its red stems and especially by its white fruit.

95

I walked down the field, holding close to the edge of the overgrown road. To my right the ground spread out in an undulating blanket of green and brown grasses dotted here and there by a dozen or more widely separated pines, none more than five to ten feet high. At the field's lower end I came to a spot where, for a span of fifteen or twenty feet, the old road completely disappeared beneath a level patch of closely cropped grass. From this opening I could see past the wild tangle of the old road and into the far field. I was somewhat surprised to find that the far corner of that field was enclosed within a wire fence. Set securely within this enclosure were two small and well maintained red barns. At this point I also realized that I was being watched. Near the red barns stood several sheep and two llamas, all seemingly transfixed by my sudden appearance. Looking more like statues than living animals, they remained motionless for the several minutes that I was in their view. At first sight this bucolic tableau, complete with enclosed pasture, barn, sheep, and llamas appeared decidedly out of place, hidden as it was within the forest. It seemed more like a vision out of a childhood fairy tale than a real place. That thought lasted only a moment before I noticed the vaporous white smoke of a wood fire filtering through trees that formed a backdrop to the animals and barns. Blending almost imperceptibly with the colors of the forest was the faint contour of a chimney and the straight lines of a gray roof. I had passed beyond the forested southern boundary of Malabar Farm and was now walking on someone's private land. Fortunately for my quest there had been no "No Trespassing" signs posted beyond the Park's edge.

I found the course of the old roadbed difficult to detect where it re-entered the woods. At this point I had two possible routes to follow. One went straight downhill and seemed to have all the characteristics I had come to expect as I had followed the old and abandoned road from Ferguson's Meadow. It was of approximately the correct width. Its banks were sloping in from years of erosion, the trees in its path appeared to be smaller than many of those beyond its edges, and it was heading down the hill in the direction that I expected the road would go. I followed this route into the woods for a short distance until it came to an abrupt end at the edge of a gaping and boulder filled gully. The gully's ragged edges were overhung by thick clusters of grass and the dangling roots of leaning trees that threatened to tumble into the ravine at any moment. The exposed earthen walls of the gully were only loosely bound together by a mesh of fine roots and assorted pebbles. Many years of heavy downpours would have been needed to produce such a gash in the landscape. I doubted that a road would have survived long had it been routed this way.

The second possible direction for the road now seemed to be the more reasonable choice. I backtracked to the field's edge and turned on to that path, which held the added attraction of continuing to follow the general direction of the gas line where it had reappeared from beneath the field. Here the lane was only moderately covered with weeds and tree sprouts. I was able to walk within it rather than along the gas line. To my dismay I soon observed that the gas line was swinging further and further west and away from the roadbed. I began to wonder if perhaps this, like the earlier option, was not the old road. I had that question answered quite abruptly when I found myself confronted with a huge, cottage-sized sandstone outcropping that lay directly across my path, blocking it from side to side. This was a great mass of stone, much of it appearing to be buried beneath the forest floor like the hidden portions of an iceberg. Its rough and weather pocked surface, matted with thick blankets of greenish and aging moss, suggested that the rock had rested here for ages. Clustered around this largest boulder were numerous smaller but still quite imposing and very permanent looking stones. I guessed that below the surface all of these outlying stones belonged to one gigantic rock formation. I looked to the left and right for any evidence that the roadbed had turned away from this obstacle. Surely anyone scouting the route of a new road would have been aware of this monolithic obstruction and would have avoided a direction that was so effectively blocked. This consideration was reinforced by the observation that the surrounding forest was free of any rocky impediments. Unfortunately, it was also free of any evidence of a continuing roadbed.

If this was not the route taken by Ferguson's Road then where was the thing? Had time and man so completely obliterated evidence of it that I would never find it? On a previous hike I had lost a river, now I had lost a road! Was my hope of following the Ferguson Highway all the way to Newville to end here, well short of my goal? I could bushwhack my way downhill, certain that I would eventually bottom out somewhere along Route 95 near Newville, but the objective of finding the town had not been the driving force behind this hike. I already knew the location of Newville. What I wanted to do was follow a long abandoned and mostly forgotten road for its entire length, to discover its opposite end at Newville. Adding spice to the adventure was the thought that such a trek had most likely not been made by anyone in nearly a century.

Somewhat discouraged, but not yet willing to give up, I decided that I should take a another look at the route that I had previously considered and abandoned. Perhaps I had been a little too hasty in judging it unfit to have once been a road. With nothing to lose that I hadn't already lost I retraced my steps through the woods and cautiously climbed into the eroded gully that I had earlier rejected as the road bed. I slowly worked my way through its ragged upper channel, scrambling around and over a jumble of loose rocks and accumulated forest debris. The going was relatively easy in spite of the unsure footing, until I came upon one especially large sandstone boulder that nearly spanned the width of the ravine. Its base was deeply undercut by years of erosion, suggesting an instability that temporarily halted my descent. With great care I managed to work my way past this final obstacle and was immediately delighted to find myself standing within a diminutive Grand Canyon, its own miniature Colorado riverbed slicing a zig-zag channel ahead of me. The constricted rush of water from countless thunderstorms had created a deep trench with steep-sided walls composed of blended layers of brown, yellow, and gray clays. Grasses, ferns, and small trees decorated the canyon's upper edges, their exposed roots dangling from the undercut ledge like badly frayed cloth.

As I pondered the real possibility that my hike ended here, I looked to my left and for the first time noticed what appeared to be a slim ledge of compacted earth extending outward along the gully's wall. This narrow shelf traced a rough line parallel to and just below the lip of the ravine. Little more than a foot wide, it followed the contour of the ravine for about thirty yards to where the gully disappeared into the surrounding forest floor. Could this modest little ledge be all that remained of the original surface of the old road? Might the abandoned road have been so thoroughly undermined by the elements that it had almost vanished? Using my walking stick for support, and with my free hand grasping at finger sized roots, I gingerly climbed up to this slender shelf. Inching sideways along it, all the while hoping it wouldn't collapse beneath me, I followed its path down to where the gully ended at what was clearly the shallow bed of an old road. I had

The old road rediscovered.

rediscovered Ferguson's Road and I don't mind saying now that I was quite pleased with my effort. My journey to Newville would continue. From this point forward I was able to walk in the road itself, the way being much less obstructed by multi-flora rose and the various trees and shrubs that had clogged so much of the road's earlier stretches.

Approaching the bottom of the hill I knew before I saw it that State Route 95 lay not far ahead. This modern road connects the small towns of Butler and Perrysville. Newville was located almost equidistant between these two villages. Long ago my abandoned road had intersected what was then called the Butler-Perrysville Road, but I wasn't sure exactly where. I continued following the old roadbed for several minutes until it began to parallel the black ribbon of a newly paved driveway that climbed the hill to my left. The drive ended at a house that lay almost hidden behind the intervening trees, probably the same house whose rooftop I had observed rising behind the sheep and llamas. In the summer this house would have been completely concealed by the thick cover of leaves. Knowing that I was on private land I left the old road and turned into the woods to avoid passing any closer to the house. Minutes later I came to another gas-line, its right-of-away making a gradual curve to my left. Following it brought me to an open grass covered clearing at the very spot where the new driveway met Route 95. Crossing the lower end of the drive I found what remained of Ferguson Road. Somewhere behind me the driveway had cut across the old roadbed. I wonder if the people who everyday use this drive know that their lane crosses this much older road. At this end of it there is nothing left of the Ferguson Road except a narrow depression, choked shut now by an impenetrable tangle of thorny rose bushes and small trees, all struggling vainly against each other for sunlight. Ferguson Road ends ignominiously where this tightly interwoven mass of vegetation meets with the closely cropped grass that lines the berm of Ohio State Route 95.

Once I had emerged onto the highway it was necessary to follow its narrow berm about a quarter of a mile southwest to reach what had once been downtown Newville. Newville, now nothing more than a ghost town, hasn't existed since the mid-1930s, when it was vacated and razed because it sat within the flood plain of the newly constructed Pleasant Hill Reservoir. A thick stand of forty to fifty foot high red pine trees now grows where downtown Newville once stood. Crossing the highway I entered the pine grove, hoping to find some evidence of the town that had once thrived there.

Unfortunately little remains. It is amazing how completely a town the size of Newville can disappear. Idid find several rectangular depressions hidden among the trees, all that remained of cellars. A few bricks lay about, and here and there a rusting bucket, not much more than crumpled rims with tattered bits of

Newville in its prime... Photograph courtesy Malabar Farm State Park

...and "downtown" Newville today.

rusting metal clinging to them. The most interesting evidence of Newville that I discovered were two stone lined wells, both about four feet in diameter. One of them had been filled in with dirt to about a foot of its top; the other went down some ten feet, bottoming out in a black and oozy muck. I also discovered a solitary standing remnant of the multitude of buildings that once had been Newville. On the south side of Bunkerhill Road, where it intersects Route 95 at what had been the center of town, there survives the collapsing remnants of an old red brick wall. Several courses of brick endure, somehow having avoided complete destruction when the town was demolished. Rectangular depressions in the ground, two mud filled wells, a couple of rotting buckets, some crumbling bricks... all that remain of Newville, lonely and silent testimony to what was once a thriving community.

I could walk the long forgotten Ferguson Road and in its choked abandonment still imagine the ghosts of the past surrounding me. However, as I stood on the former site of Newville the town had been so successfully erased that I couldn't conjure up even shadowy images of its former occupants. Their homes and places of work had been so altogether obliterated that nothing was left to work with save two wells, some rusting buckets, a few bricks, and an old black and white photograph, and those were not enough. A friend told me that years ago he had seen a small history of Newville, possibly a self-published book. It had included additional photographs, but he couldn't remember where he had seen it, and hadn't been able to find it since. Newville is gone, only a rapidly fading memory, only a black dot alongside a name on ancient, yellowing maps. But once upon a time it had had a life.

The town of Newville was located on the banks of the Clear Fork River. It had been founded in 1823 by John Herring, who operated a grist mill on the river. Herring named the town after Newville, Pennsylvania, his former home. Because of John Herring's mill Newville grew quickly and soon boasted not only the mill but also a tavern, a general store, and a blacksmith shop. In time a hardware store was established and a doctor opened an office in town. So successful was Newville that it even competed with Mansfield to become the Richland County seat. Losing this competition seems to have established a pattern of disappointments that the town would experience in the coming years. In the mid-nineteenth century railroads came to southern Richland County. First there was the Baltimore and Ohio. It went through Butler five miles southwest of Newville. Next came the Pennsylvania Railroad. It went through Perrysville five miles to the northeast. Newville found itself stranded between the two rail lines, and, as so often happened when towns were bypassed by the railroads, it began to slowly wither.

By the early 20th century, Newville, once a promising center for agricultural commerce, had become a shell of its former self. Where once there had been several hundred residents, now fewer than a hundred remained. When the Army Corp of Engineers completed building the Pleasant Hill Reservoir, one of many such flood control projects at the time, it was determined that Newville was within the flood plain of the reservoir. The few dozen people still living there were relocated and in 1936 the town was razed to the ground. Within a decade or two even the huge, rough cut sandstone blocks that had served as foundations and cellar walls for the stores and houses of Newville had been carted away to form the foundations, garden walls, and chimneys of new homes.[8]

Most people speeding along Route 95, past the intersection of Bunkerhill Road, past the grove of tall red pines, have no idea that a town once existed here. Almost nothing remains that might alert them to Newville's former existence. The Newville Baptist Church still endures, and one can still drive the Butler-Newville Road. These are about all that a passing motorist is likely to notice. Out of sight from the highway, however, there is one additional remnant of Newville, and this one is without question the town's most poignant survivor. On the northern side of the highway, on a hillside overlooking the tall pines, rests the old Newville Cemetery. I only discovered this site by accident. With nothing left to be seen of Newville I decided to explore a short side road that enters Route 95 opposite Bunkerhill Road. Only a few hundred yards in length, the road climbs the hillside a short distance, then loops back to the highway. The center of the loop is dominated by a small grove of walnut trees. Several small houses line the circle's outer rim. Most of the homes appear to be relatively new arrivals, but one or two are older, possibly survivors from the ghost town below. Nestled in among these homes I came upon the old cemetery, its small gravestones scattered among a few scraggly shrubs and ancient trees. Though it appears that the grass is being cut on a regular basis, many of the aged and weather-worn markers, none of them bearing any particular grandeur, lean at odd angles. With the weight of history pressing down upon them these crooked gray stones endure, though now enshrouded with a sad and forlorn aura.

Newville Cemetery

Something of the history of Newville resides in the many names that remain legible on the stones in this small burial ground. Resting here is Hiram Carpenter, only 17 years of age when he died and was buried in 1832. Hiram's stone carries the earliest burial date that remains legible in the cemetery, though there are other gravestones that are too badly worn to be read. The last burial to take place here happened years after Newville had been razed. In 1948 eighty-three year old John Taylor was buried beside his wife Ida, who had died in 1900. Ida was only thirty-three years old when she died. At her side rest the remains of twin newborn daughters. Dying in child-birth remained a leading cause of death for women at that time. Perhaps this was Ida's fate. It would be forty-eight years before an elderly John Taylor would join his wife and daughters in the Newville Cemetery. I couldn't find the graves of W. and S. Capler in the cemetery, but their names do stand out prominently on a series of four tombstones not their own. Resting in a neat row, these markers have their own tragic story to tell. William Capler died in 1841 at the age of three; his sister Mary Ann died in 1842 at age ten. Next came Wesley Capler, his age illegible. He died in 1846. The last stone in the line is that of Sarah A. Capler, age four, who died in 1848.

The markers for all four children identify them as the sons and daughters of "W&S Capler." This father and mother had had to endure the deaths of four children in a span of only seven years. Perhaps they had found it too painful to remain in Newville and had moved on, to die and be buried elsewhere.

I found one tombstone in the Newville Cemetery that is of added historic note. This weathered gray stone marks the grave of a gentleman named Adam Wolfe, who died on April 16, 1845 at the age of eighty-four years. On his stone Adam is identified as a veteran of the Revolutionary War. Later I did some research and discovered that Adam Wolfe had been born on December 16, 1760 in Beaver County, Pennsylvania and was indeed a veteran of the Revolutionary War. In 1778, at the age of eighteen, he served as a private in Captain James Wright's Company of the "Youghegenia Militia." In 1780 he served as a private with Captain Peter Fort's Company of the York Militia. There was additional service during the war, but those records have been lost. On January 16, 1790 Adam married Rachel Oldham, together they had ten children. Unlike those of the unfortunate Capler family, all ten of the Wolfe children lived to maturity and married. In 1815 Adam and Rachel left Pennsylvania, moving to the Pinhook area of southeastern Richland County.[9] From Pinhook the Wolfe's relocated to Newville, where Adam was the primary organizing influence in the founding of the Newville Baptist Church in 1825. Rachel Wolfe died on April 19, 1836 and was buried in the Newville Cemetery. Unfortunately her grave is now unmarked, though it is likely that Adam, who died only nine years later, was buried near her.

Leaving the cemetery I retraced my route back to Malabar Farm. During the walk I began to muse upon what I had discovered. William Ferguson, with his furs, his pioneer farm, and his sunken road; the ghost town of Newville with its frontier settlers, its Capler children's graves, and its Revolutionary War veteran... all had passed into the dim, shadow filled vale of history. I thought of how it has become so very easy in the rush of our technology enhanced days to forget that these individuals and the things they built even existed, too easy to forget the stories and events that form the foundations that our lives rest upon. We rush through our days, eyes narrowly focused on some future goal. We dismiss as irrelevant the past and the people who have brought us to this point. We seem oblivious to the fact that our life in the twenty-first century is the direct result of decisions made by others in the past. Who we are today as a people and a nation has been sculpted by those who proceeded us. Should we choose to acknowledge it or not, we are the descendants of yesterday and the ancestors of tomorrow. Our actions today will join with those of our forerunners in shaping the future.

Perhaps I was reflecting on the past too much, perhaps not, such was the nature of my thinking while on my long walk home up Ferguson's Road.

# Chapter 4

# Crossing Fields, Forests, and Frontiers

In 1940 Louis Bromfield purchased a seventy acre parcel of forested land that bordered the far eastern reaches of Malabar Farm. Switzer Creek flowed through this ground and lying within its heart was a marshy and cattail filled wetland. Bromfield called this parcel "The Jungle," and he left it untouched by either saw or plow. It was to remain the untrammeled home of deer, wildflowers, and songbirds. Today a narrow foot path, The Louis Bromfield Junglebrook Trail, loops through the middle of this small gem of the Malabar landscape. Enclosed within the borders of this seventy acre world, the greatest variety of wild environments can be found at Malabar Farm. Here one can explore a riparian landscape, a marsh, even a slender hillside strip of dry upland woods. The trailhead for the Junglebrook Trail can be found near the far eastern end of the one-way farm lane that bisects the central fields and pastures of Malabar Farm.

Although a small parking area sits at the trailhead itself, parking at the barn complex near the beginning of the farm lane is also an option. The dirt lane through the heart of Malabar Farm is itself a delight to walk. Coupling it with the Junglebrook Trail makes a hike of approximately two and a half miles that is one of the best and most varied walks that Malabar Farm has to offer. Not only can hikers experience the diversity found on the Junglebrook Trail, but they can also enjoy some of the most beautiful farmland in Ohio on the lane leading to the trail. Strolling is the only way to travel here; this is one hike you should never take in haste. With a little imagination to guide your thoughts, an unhurried amble down this dirt road will transport you back in time to the beginnings of the 19th century and the days of earliest settlers in this part of Ohio.

It was a sun-filled blue sky morning in late April when I decided to take the hike described here. This has always been one of my favorite places to walk at Malabar Farm. Over the years I have spent many pleasant and leisurely hours ambling along the farm lane and the Junglebrook Trail. On this occasion however I wanted to more attentively focus on the two distinctly contrasting worlds that one can experience at Malabar Farm; the untended natural environment, and the man-made one. I wanted to walk the Junglebrook Trail with eyes and mind attuned to exploring and savoring the greening and untrammeled environment of a springtime woods and wetland. However, before entering the wilder world of the nature trail, I wanted to pass some quiet time contemplating the life and times of the early pioneers who farmed this land long ago, individuals who entered a wilderness to make a life for themselves on land that 150 years later Louis Bromfield would make famous as Malabar Farm.

After the farm lane leaves the collection of buildings called Malabar's "working farm" it passes alongside a small grassy enclosure on the right. This morning it was filled with the recently born calves of polled Herefords and Baldys (a Hereford and Angus mix). Their big brown, marble-like eyes focused curiously on me as I walked by. The mothers of these calves, accustomed to seeing Park visitors, continued to eat grass, paying me little mind. On average Malabar Farm keeps a herd of forty to fifty beef cattle, mostly a mixed breed of Black Angus, Hereford, and Short-Horn and each spring the farm welcomes thirty or more new calves. On the opposite side of the lane from the cows a broad field is set aside for growing lush grasses. A combination of timothy, orchard grass, and red clover, this grass is cut and baled to provide winter food for the cattle. Louis Bromfield wrote that this region of Ohio was ideal for growing good quality grasses, and that the job of Malabar Farm was to turn that grass into beef and milk. Today Malabar limits its cattle herd to beef cattle, having ceased its dairy operations in the early 1990s.

East of the calf enclosure sits a larger pasture that the cows are released into when their calves are older. The farm lane climbs a low hill as it runs alongside this pasture, dividing it from

"The Working Farm", Malabar Farm State Park.

the broad expanse of grassland that in late spring blankets the rolling landscape in undulating waves of green that end only at the field's northern boundary of Pleasant Valley Road. A row of trees borders the pasture side of the lane as it climbs the low hill. Among these trees are several tall sycamores. On this sunny spring morning the sycamore's mottled white and green trunks were glowing in the morning's new sun. Below the trees, scattered among the grasses, weeds, and exposed roots were tiny purple droplets, the velvety flowers of ground ivy. These and the many other spring wildflowers I hoped to see in the "Jungle" were one of the primary motivations prompting this day's hike.

Too often in our harried and technology crowded days we forget to look down, reticent to pause for even a few moments to see the wonders that lay at our feet. William Blake, writing two hundred years ago in the midst of the social turmoil of England's Industrial Revolution understood this quite well, expressing it perfectly when he wrote:

110

*"To see a World in a grain of Sand*
*And Heaven in a Wild Flower..."*

Ralph Waldo Emerson, experiencing the upheavals of America's Industrial Revolution nearly a century later, also understood this, writing that:

*"Earth Laughs in Flowers"*

When artist Georgia O'Keeffe (1887-1986) was questioned about why she painted her images of flowers so large she offered a two-part explanation. First, she said that many artists could paint flowers that were as good or even better, than hers. Consequently she needed something that would make her work stand out, so she painted flowers larger than anyone else. In doing this she revealed the elegant inner workings of flowers in a way that no one else had ever done. This fulfilled O'Keeffe's second objective, to have people stop, if only for a moment, to take notice of the small things that are rarely seen and appreciated. O'Keeffe, like Emerson and Blake before her, understood the importance of being witness to the smaller details of nature. It was in nature's minute and elemental world of shape, line, and color that one could observe some of the grandest workings of creation.

Where the lane levels off at the top of the low hill it passes alongside a small copse of trees. Nestled within these trees is a

Olivet Cemetery, Malabar Farm State Park.

white picket fence that encloses a burial ground. This graveyard dates back some 200 years to the earliest pioneer days of Pleasant Valley. Olivet Cemetery has had several names. At one time it was called Pioneer Cemetery. Before that it was known as the Schrack Cemetery. It is the final resting place for Louis Bromfield, his wife, his mother and father, and a sister. The first person to be buried in Olivet Cemetery was Sarah Schrack. Sarah came to Ohio with her son David and his family in 1819. Already ill when she made the journey to Ohio from Pennsylvania Sarah died of consumption in 1821 at the age of sixty-eight. Buried near her are David and a second son Charles. Both men played very prominent roles in the early development of what would, a hundred and fifty years later, become Malabar Farm, located in Monroe Township, Richland County, Ohio.

Historians typically limit their attention to the great political, military, religious and technological events that define the times that they study. Presidents, kings, and generals, business tycoons, inventors, explorers and adventurers all get their due, quite often in great detail. However, the vast majority of individuals, those whose cooperation was necessary to the making of history, as well those countless and unfortunate souls who were helplessly swept along in its wake, have been forgotten. Olivet Cemetery shelters the remains of men and women who for the most part have been lost to time. Even the stones that mark their passing are now nearly illegible. It was their courage, perseverance, and imagination, as well as that of George Washington and Thomas Jefferson, Meriwether Lewis and William Clark, Robert Fulton and Cyrus McCormick, that built the American nation. In the day-to-day living of their lives these people wove the fabric of a cultural and physical environment the threads of which continue today in these thousand acres called Malabar Farm. By telling their stories and relating their contributions to our collective American history I hope that in some small way they will stand for their countless brothers and sisters now unknown and unknowable. I also hope that in gaining this knowledge your future walks along Malabar Farm's earthen lane and forested trails will be enriched.

Ohio became a State in 1803. Richland County was formed only five years later. In 1813 Richland County was divided into four townships, Madison, Jefferson, Vermillion, and Green, with Green Township occupying the southeastern quarter of the county. Richland County experienced slow but steady growth until the War of 1812 halted most emigration into the region. The signing of the Treaty of Ghent on December 24, 1814 ended the war and emigration resumed. Soon new settlers were flooding into Richland County to carve out homes in what was then still largely a wilderness. These pioneers, many of them from Pennsylvania, had served as soldiers in the Ohio country. Liking what they saw they returned, bringing their families with them. Military roads that had been cut into the region for the use of armies, facilitated this migration into the wilds of Ohio. Until the coming of the railroads in mid-century these rough roads were the only means of transportation and communication between the early settlers of southern Richland County and the outside world.

With an expanding population Green Township was divided into two parts in 1815. The western half of the Township was named Worthington Township after Thomas Worthington, governor of Ohio at the time.[10] As its population continued to expand, Worthington Township was itself divided in 1817, the northern half becoming Monroe Township.

David Schrack purchased his land in Monroe Township in 1817 but didn't move his family fromCenter County, Pennsylvania until 1819. Located on his new Ohio land was a large spring of clear, fresh water that had been flowing from the base of a sandstone cliff for as long as the few Indians who remained in the area could remember. The advantages offered by this spring motivated David's purchase of this particular parcel of land. At the time of his arrival much of Monroe Township was still densely covered with a virgin forest. It took many weeks and months of back-breaking labor to clear enough ground to begin planting. In many places trees were cut and the first crops planted around the stumps. Removal of the stumps would have to come later. David also built a cabin for his family, using logs from the land that he had cleared. He chose as the site for his cabin an expanse of level ground that was sheltered below the rocky hillside out of which flowed his big spring.

With his land cleared and his farm in operation David quickly turned his considerable energies to the building of a more suitable home for his family.[11] In 1822, using bricks fired on the site, he built the large multiple story home that still stands today. Located only yards from the spring, this former farmhouse now serves as the Malabar Farm Restaurant. Louis Bromfield wrote of wanting to establish a restaurant in the old Schrack home but died before that could happen. His dream was fulfilled on July 1, 1963 when Agnes Schwartz signed a lease with the Louis Bromfield Malabar Farm Foundation to operate a restaurant in the old brick house, naming it "The Malabar Inn." That restaurant closed about sixteen months later, but was re-opened under new management

114

in July of 1965, and has remained open ever since.

Bromfield, possibly in an attempt to create a "romantic" history for his future restaurant, wrote that David Schrack operated a stagecoach stop out of his home, ministering to the needs of travelers on a busy highway that connected Lake Erie to the Ohio River. Unfortunately, no evidence exists for this claim beyond the words of Bromfield himself. Neither Findley's pocket map of Ohio, produced in 1830, nor Mitchell's Ohio map of 1839 show a major road passing near the location of David Schrack's home. Perhaps David did give shelter to the occasional traveler, but not as an innkeeper on a busy road.

David Schrack died in 1861 at the age of seventy-six. He was buried near his mother Sarah. His son Charles inherited the farm. When Louis Bromfield bought this land it was still referred to as the old Schrack Place, although it was no longer owned by the Schrack family. Bromfield restored the aging red brick homestead, using it to house farm workers and over-flow farm guests. In the 1950's he built a concrete produce stand that utilized the chilled spring water as a natural refrigerant. Icy cold water was directed into cascading troughs where it flowed only inches beneath wooden racks heaped with vegetables and fruits. As it had been in Indian and pioneer days this spring became during Bromfield's time a gathering place for friends, neighbors and passers-by.

*"And so our spring and fountain and market stand, here in the middle of Ohio have become, like fountains everywhere, a gathering place in the heat of the day and in the long blue evenings when neighbors and friends drift in to talk to the sound of the spring water falling from trough to trough among the fresh green vegetables and fruit."*

− Louis Bromfield,
*From My Experience,* 1955

Only a few feet away from David's marker is the grave of

115

his brother Charles Schrack. Born in Pennsylvania in 1788, Charles was three years younger than David. Charles and his family followed David to Ohio in 1819. Charles had gained some experience working in a grist mill while living in Pennsylvania. Seeing how hard his brother was working to clear land for farming, he chose a different vocational path. At first he constructed and operated a small grist and saw mill on Switzer

The Charles Schrack home, c1915 photograph courtesy Malabar Farm State Park

Creek, about three quarters of a mile west of David's farm, locating it just behind and below the site of the current Malabar Farm Hostel. Around 1830 Charles expanded his operation, building a much larger three story mill on the creek. He also built his family a large frame house that stood on the ground where the hostel now stands. Charles Schrack died in 1860 at the age of seventy-two. The site of the Charles Schrack mill, which was dismantled and carted away in 1919, was on land that Louis Bromfield purchased in 1939 to create Malabar Farm. Although the structure itself was long gone, the foundation stones for the mill were still there. Bromfield had these massive sandstone blocks removed to his new home, using them to create part of the retaining walls of the terraced flower gardens that still grace the south side of Malabar's Big House.

In a row of tombstones that faces Sarah Schrack's stone there sits a weathered gray marker that reads *William Ferguson d 17 Feb 1851 75-1-8*. William Ferguson was one on the earliest white men to establish roots in the land that would later be named Malabar Farm. Born in 1776 in Cumberland County, Pennsylvania he first entered the southern Richland County area around 1805, several years before the county existed. He came to the Ohio country to trade for furs with the Delaware (Lenape) Indians who were still living in the area. In the first decade of the 19th century no roads led into the region and William most likely walked the old Wyondot Indian Trail that followed the Black Fork River and the Clear Fork River to the Mohican River and beyond. This pathway through the wilderness connected Lake Erie with the site where the Monongahela and Allegheny Rivers come together to form the Ohio River at what is now Pittsburgh, Pennsylvania. During that first decade of the new century, William Ferguson made annual trips to the region, eventually building a log cabin on the south side of a ridge high above where the Malabar Farm Sugar Shack now sits.

By the early years of the 19th century the fur trade was collapsing east of the Mississippi River, the once rich stock of fur bearing animals having been depleted. William Ferguson came in on the end of this enterprise and likely didn't prosper for very long. He did, however, find the wild Ohio country that surrounded his cabin to his liking. In 1815 he moved his family to land that had been named Richland County only seven years earlier. Coming with him were his wife Jane, his father-in-law, and his three children, fifteen year old Elizabeth, ten year old Mary, and eight year old John.[12] William cleared land for farming on flat ground on the hilltop above his cabin. The family lived a somewhat primitive existence in the cabin for a number of years before William built a two story frame house and converted the old cabin into a barn. Eventually his son John Ferguson took over operation of the farm.

John sold the land to his son Isaac Ferguson in 1891. In 1922 Isaac sold the property to Clement Herring, who was related to the Fergusons. When Louis Bromfield began his Malabar Farm adventure with the purchase of the Clement Herring farm in January of 1939 the old Ferguson farm was part of the purchase. Sadly, William Ferguson's frame house was no longer standing, having burned down some time earlier, but remnants of William Ferguson's ancient log cabin could still be seen.[13] Today those rotted and crumbling remains of the log cabin have disappeared into the soil. All that survives of the William Ferguson farm are a few scattered chimney bricks, the concrete steps that led to the front porch of the second Ferguson home, and the depression of a cellar located some twenty feet behind the steps. Even these traces are now nearly lost among the trees and briers that have taken over the former Ferguson Homestead.

Much of the farmland that the Fergusons cleared those many years ago still remains open, being maintained as a meadow by Malabar Farm staff. Once used by Louis Bromfield as pasture for his cattle, this high area of the Park is accessible via a portion of the old Ferguson Road (see chapter 3). Now known as Ferguson's Meadow, it is a broad open field of tall grasses, speckled by small clusters of trees and shrubs. The meadow is bordered on the south by a dark woods of red pines. The north side is framed by a mixed forest and a scattering of aged and gnarled apple trees. Ferguson's Meadow was perhaps Louis Bromfield's best-loved locale on his farm. Open to the sky, yet remote from the remainder of the farm, the meadow offered a place of solitude, a place to think and unwind from the stresses of the day. It was understood that, if in the cool of the evening someone was seen climbing the hill to the meadow he or she was to be left alone to wander untroubled by the need to explain themselves.

*The house was burned long ago...but the ghostly touch of man's hand is still there... This is the Ferguson place, a beautiful, wild, and haunted farm.*

– Louis Bromfield, *Pleasant Valley,* 1945

Louis Bromfield died on March 18, 1956. He was the last person to be buried in Olivet Cemetery. He was a veteran of the First World War, having served as an ambulance driver, first for the French Army and later as a private in the United States Army. Annually on Memorial Day a new American flag is placed on his grave. On that same day a second flag is placed on another grave not far from Bromfield's. Resting beneath that second flag is a Civil War soldier named George Franklin Baughman. Baughman had served for only six months when he died of dysentery on March 24, 1863. George Baughman's brief military career paralleled that of tens of thousands of young men who lost their lives to disease rather than bullets during the four long years of the American Civil War. The story of the Baughman family reflects the restless movements of millions of Europeans who immigrated to America in the 18th and 19th centuries.

George was the great-grandson of Abraham Baughman of Wurttemberg, Germany. Abraham and his then pregnant wife immigrated to the United States in the late 18th century, sometime around 1790. Their son Abraham Jr. was born on the ship while still in transit on the Atlantic Ocean. The Baughmans first settled in the Cumberland Valley of Pennsylvania. In 1803 the family moved west to Washington County, Pennsylvania. From Pennsylvania they moved to Ohio around 1807 settling along the Clearfork River, near present day Perrysville, Ohio five miles northeast of today's Malabar Farm. In 1812 the Baughman clan moved once again, this time to what would soon become Monroe Township in Richland County. Aaron Baughman, son of Abraham Jr. was the third generation Baughman to live in the United States, but the first to be born on American soil. He married Catherine Schrack, the daughter of David Schrack. Their son George, was born on April 26, 1840.[14]

George Franklin Baughman, a twenty-two-year-old farmer at the time, enlisted in the Union army in the late summer of 1862, the second year of the Civil War. He married Margaret L. Morris on September 25, 1862 and only three weeks later was mustered into Company B of the 120th Ohio Volunteer Infantry. The 120th soon became part of the right wing of the Army of Tennessee. In late December George fought in the battles of Chickasaw Bayou and Chickasaw Bluffs. These engagements opened Major General Ulysses Grant's campaign to capture Vicksburg and gain control of the Mississippi River. Both engagements were unmitigated disasters for Grant and his army. Union casualties; dead, wounded, or missing numbered over 4,050, the Confederates only 500.

During the second week of January, 1863 George was with the 120th OVI in Arkansas at the battle of Fort Hindman on the Mississippi River. This was also part of Grant's push on Vicksburg, being fought this time to stop Confederate harassment of Union shipping and lines of communication. This battle was much more successful than the earlier debacles in Mississippi, and significantly raised Union morale. Also known as the Battle of Arkansas Post, Fort Hindman was surrounded and forced to surrender on January 11. Federal losses included 134 killed, 898 wounded, and 29 missing. The Confederates, protected within their fort, lost fewer men, with 60 killed and 80 wounded, but were forced to surrender 4,791 men. This was a quarter of the Confederate forces in Arkansas and a serious blow to the South.

George Baughman survived all three of these battles, apparently uninjured, but couldn't survive the disease that struck him down soon after. Three out of every five soldier deaths during the Civil War were the result of disease. In early March George fell victim to dysentery, a severe inflammation of his intestines. He died on March 24, 1863, having been a soldier for only six months. Initially interred in the cemetery at Jefferson Barracks in St. Louis, he was later reburied in the Schrack Cemetery near the fields that he had farmed.

The last pioneer profile I will offer here is that of John Tucker. He was one of Monroe Township's early settlers and one of its more eccentric individuals. John Tucker isn't buried in the Olivet cemetery, but four of his grandchildren are. Laura Tucker was only twenty-two days old at the time of her death in 1851. Lillie Tucker was just ten months old when she died in 1860. Sarah Tucker died in 1867 at six months of age. Their brother William Tucker's marker is partially missing and lacks a date. All four gravestones identify the children as the daughters and son of A & I, the A. and I. on the stones are for Aurelius Tucker and his wife Isabella. Aurelius Tucker, born in Monroe Township in 1828, was the son of John Tucker.

At the age of nineteen in 1816, John Tucker, seeking his fortune, left his home in Hillsborough County, New Hampshire and headed west on foot. He stopped walking when he reached Terre Haute, Indiana, which in the early years of the nineteenth century consisted of little more than a fort and a single home. After a time, having not discovered the opportunities there that he had hoped for, Tucker returned east. By 1818 he had made his way to Richland County, Ohio, again having traveled the entire distance on foot. Here Tucker cleared land in Monroe Township and built a cabin, then returned to New Hampshire, where in 1821 he married Mary Ward. Shortly after their wedding the couple loaded their belongings onto a one-horse wagon and headed for John's cabin in Ohio. Once settled into their new home Tucker began farming. In the winter he taught school. As Monroe Township had no schools at the time, and all of Richland County only a few such facilities, Tucker found it necessary to travel east to Stark County to secure a teaching position.

In addition to farming and teaching, John Tucker was also something of a pioneer doctor, practicing a healing method called the Thomsonian System. This system of alternative medicine, named after its New Hampshire originator a self-taught herbalist named Samuel Thomson (1769-1843), enjoyed wide spread popularity during the 19th century. Samuel Thomson had acquired his early education in medicinal plants from a local woman who had a reputation as a healer. Thomson married in 1790, and when his wife suffered an undefined illness following the birth of their first child conventional doctors were unable to provide relief. Remembering his earlier experiences Thomson secured the services of two "root doctors," who restored her to health in a single day. Impressed with the results provided by these individuals Thomson began to study with the two herbalists who taught him many of their methods. During the next several years, Thomson developed and refined the system that would be named after him. In essence the Thomsonian System consisted of opening pathways for the removal of toxins from the body. Thomson believed that long exposure to cold temperatures was a contributing cause for most maladies. He believed that these ailments could be treated and cured by reestablishing what he called the body's "natural heat." His system accomplished this by the use of steam baths, cayenne pepper, laxatives, and the emetic Lobelia inflata, an herb known generally as Indian tobacco or puke weed.

Feeling threatened by the growing popularity of Thomson's methods licensed doctors began to protest and managed to pressure many States into passing so called "black laws" that limited the practice of unconventional medical systems like that of Thomson. In a reflection of the times, these laws had come to be called black laws by their adversaries, who likened them to laws of the day that prevented blacks from practicing medicine. Rarely enforced, most black laws were repealed by the 1820s.

In 1822, freed from even the slight fear of legal prosecution, Thomson published his *New Guide To Health: A*

*Botanical Family Physician.* This volume soon became a bible of sorts for the alternative medicine industry. Thomson also sold his system of medicine in the form of medical "patents." For a fee of $20 one could secure the right to purchase Thomson's herbs and formulas. By 1840 Samuel Thomson, the self-taught herbalist, was a wealthy man, having sold more than 100,000 of these patents. One on his most ardent followers was John Tucker of Monroe Township, Richland County, Ohio.

In addition to his allegiance to alternative medicine John Tucker was something of a religious rebel. While most of the residents of Richland County were content to follow the traditional tenets of the Lutheran, Baptist, Presbyterian, or Congregational Church, Tucker was an early and devout believer in the Swedenborgian doctrine. Emanuel Swedenborg (1688-1772) was a Swedish scientist, philosopher, and theologian. At the age of fifty-three, with a distinguished career behind him, Swedenborg began to experience dreams and visions that resulted in a spiritual awakening in which he claimed that he had been chosen to write a doctrine that would remake Christianity. He also said that in these visions God had allowed him to visit both heaven and hell and to communicate with the inhabitants of those realms, both angelic and demonic. In what was to become Swedenborg's most controversial claim he stated that the Last Judgment had taken place in 1757, and that it was not a physical event but rather a spiritual one. He knew this because he had witnessed it. This final judgment had then been followed by the Second Coming of Christ, also to be experienced not as an actual physical return, but rather realized in the inner spiritual sense of the Word. In claims that raised many eyebrows in his day Swedenborg also rejected the Church's doctrine of the trinity, saying that there was no Biblical support for such an idea and that the early Christian Church never taught such a three-part divinity.

Swedenborg believed that the Bible expressed man's transformation from a physical to a spiritual being, something that he called regeneration. Although he never attempted to establish his own church for the last twenty-eight years of his life Swedenborg wrote and published eighteen theological works explaining his beliefs. He never referred to these writings as theological works because he claimed that they were based on his own actual experiences. In 1784 James Glen, an Englishman with land holdings in South America, brought the Swedenborgian doctrine to the Americas. Within twenty years the first Swedenborg Church had been established in the United States. By 1787, fifteen years after his death, followers of Swedenborg in London had established the Church of the New Jerusalem, dedicated to promoting his religious ideas.

Different though his beliefs may have been from the great majority of his Monroe Township neighbors, John Tucker wasn't alone in his interest in the teachings of Emanuel Swedenborg. A list of culturally prominent individuals influenced by the work of the Swedish mystic would eventually come to include the following: William Blake, Arthur Conan Doyle, Ralph Waldo Emerson, George Inness, Carl Jung, Immanuel Kant, Helen Keller, W. B. Yeats, and that fellow Ohio eccentric, the much loved gentleman named John Chapman, better known as Johnny Appleseed.

In 1838, twenty years after first walking there, John Tucker returned to Indiana where he purchased 1,600 acres of farm land in Kosciusko County. In 1846 he walked all the way to Missouri to see land but didn't like what he found and soon returned to Ohio. In 1853 he sold his Monroe Township farm to his son Aurelius and moved with his wife to his land in Indiana. John Tucker died on Christmas Day in 1879 at the age of 82 and was buried in Palestine, Indiana. Aurelius Tucker died in 1897, and his wife Isabella in 1894, both are buried in the Pleasant Valley Cemetery, about three-quarters of a mile up the Pleasant Valley Road from Malabar Farm. Nothing has been written about Aurelius Tucker's medical or religious beliefs, but he did become a breeder of prize winning horses.

Stepping through the tall gasses and amid the gray and lichen encrusted stones of Olivet Cemetery I drifted into a dream-like musing upon the lives of the Bromfield family, of William Ferguson, of the Schrack brothers, of George Baughman, and of the young children of Aurelius and Isabella Tucker. Enveloped in this reflective mood, my attention was drawn to the hushed voice of a soft wind as it passed through the highest branches of surrounding trees, communicating in a language far more ancient than the oldest stone at my feet. The blue sky was dappled with cotton ball clouds, crossed and re-crossed by the frenetic darting of swallows and the more graceful aerial dance of a pair of bluebirds. It is said that Sarah Schrack herself chose this particular ground for her final resting place, she chose well.

Being in a reflective mood, my thoughts turned to something I had recently read about John Muir, author, naturalist, outspoken defender of wilderness, and co-founder of the Sierra Club. In September of 1867 Muir began a thousand mile walk that eventually took him from Indiana to the Gulf of Mexico. On this trek he chose the wildest and least traveled routes that he could find. By the time Muir reached Savannah, Georgia funds were running low and he was unable to afford even the cheapest lodging. Being unfamiliar with black people he admitted to fearing them. He had, however, been told by locals that blacks where afraid of ghosts. Believing this Muir decided to take shelter beneath the long skeins of Spanish Moss that hung from the branches of an aged oak tree in a cemetery on the grounds of an abandoned 18th century mansion. From this vantage point he noted several new stones among the ancient monuments. These new markers brought to Muir's mind the horrific loss of countless young lives during the recently ended Civil War.

Brooding over the seeming incongruity between the weathered and grim monuments to death, the lush greenery and colorful flowers that surrounded and covered the graves, and the lively flight of many birds overhead, Muir wrote that here, among the cold stones, the bright flowers, and the flitting birds he began to consider that in spite of its stated purpose the cemetery was in fact "a center of life." In his notebooks from this time Muir begins to question the tenants of a Calvinist Christianity as it had been defined by his strict and abusive father. As he matured, John Muir came to acknowledge no conflict between life and death. He recognized both as parts of an eternal cycle. Following his brief sojourn in a derelict Savannah graveyard for John Muir cemeteries would no longer generate those dark and discomforting thoughts that so many other people experience in such environs.

Leaving Olivet Cemetery the farm lane follows a serpentine route between fields and pastures before straightening out and running along the northern edge of Malabar woodlands. On this spring morning a curious red winged blackbird skipped

along fence posts, keeping just far enough ahead of me to preclude a quick photograph. It was almost as though he was playing a game. I would raise my camera and he would skip ahead to the next post, then turn to look back at me. Overhead several turkey vultures soared, their broad wings catching invisible currents. They circled in graceful and ever widening spirals, first overhead, then drifting away south and out of sight beyond a distant ridge.

In April the forest that runs alongside the lane is subtly accented with hundreds of the white, sunlit blossoms of dogwood trees. A few of these decorative understory trees display their finery along the edge of the lane, many others hide their beauty deeper within the surrounding forest, their flowers appearing like great snowflakes floating serenely among the somber browns and grays of the trees that surround them. Opposite this woods is a wide field that is typically planted in a rotation of corn, soy beans, and occasionally oats. This early in the season the field is bare, blanketed only with the bristly stubble of last year's corn crop, as much an expression of anticipation as an example of rich cropland. Beyond this field, and serving as a dramatic backdrop, rises the grass covered slopes and open summit of Mount Jeez. Some people claim that the top of Mt. Jeez is the highest point in Richland County, others dispute this claim, but it is certainly the

Mt. Jeez in the background, Malabar Farm State Park.

highest point in Monroe Township. A narrow, winding, and rutted dirt road climbs the hill leading to a small parking area on its flat top. From here Malabar Farm and Pleasant Valley spread out before one in a stunning panoramic vision of field, pasture, and forest that equals the best of Englishman John Constable's bucolic landscapes and the most dramatic nature paintings of America's own Hudson River School.

Mount Jeez was part of the original David Schrack farm. Purchased in 1942 that farm was the last of the farms bought by Louis Bromfield. The Schrack family no longer owned the land, though their name was still often associated with it. Now owned by a man named Neiman this land had been leased to others for many years before Bromfield bought it. It was the most neglected and abused of the properties that he would acquire. For decades prior to Bromfield's coming the high hill on the old Schrack place had been mockingly referred to as Poverty Knob. In *Pleasant Valley* (1945) Bromfield wrote of tenant farmers who had plowed up and down its steep sides for years, eventually resulting in eroded gullies so deep that you could lose a team of horses in them. One of Bromfield's first jobs after buying the land was to fill in the gullies and replant the hillsides with good quality grasses that would hold the soil in place and prevent future erosion. Today, in keeping with Bromfield's conservation program, the lush high grasses of Mount Jeez's slopes provide hay and grazing for cattle. No plow touches the soil.

The trailhead for Louis Bromfield's Junglebrook Trail, a one mile loop that traverses some of the most diverse environments in the Park, begins where the farm lane makes a horseshoe curve that ends in a line heading northeast toward Pleasant Valley Road. As I left the farm lane and stepped onto the wooded Junglebrook Trail I turned my back to the world of fences and barns, the world of corn and soybean fields, to enter a much different springtime world, a world that is at once both forever ancient and forever being reborn. By late April the forest's floor is carpeted with May apples, or witch's umbrellas as they were known in past days.[15] Scattered widely among the May apples are the pink flowers of wild geraniums and the more profusely occurring confetti-like blossoms of blue phlox, their petals giving the appearance of jeweled fragments of the sky, fallen to earth and stitched into a green crazy quilt of thousands of tiny parasol leaves of the May apples. This alone would have made my walk through Louis Bromfield's Jungle worthwhile, but it was only the beginning.

Once into the woods I followed the trail gently downhill towards Switzer Creek, the pathway surrounded by red oak, basswood, black cherry, and a smattering of shag-bark hickory, the hoary old men of the forest. Scattered here and there were young buckeye trees, leaves just emerging, but oddly enough I could find no mature buckeyes. At my feet, clustered in small bunches among the spring-green grasses that grow along the trail's edge, were purple wild violets, with a few yellow and white ones thrown in for variety.

According to Greek mythology we have Zeus to thank for these gems of the forest floor. As the story goes Zeus had something of a roving eye, a condition complicated by the jealousies of his consort Hera. While on one of his many wanderings Zeus came upon a comely maiden named Io, the daughter of a river god. As was his nature Zeus proceeded to seduce her. Fearing Hera's wrath should she discover this latest of his indiscretions, and wishing to keep lovely Io all to himself, Zeus transformed the girl into a beautiful white heifer and then hid her away in one of his distant pastures.

On a future day Zeus went out in search of Io, but for the longest time could not find her. Finally he came upon her, hidden away in the most remote part of the most far-flung of his pastures and she was crying. Although Io tried to hide her weeping Zeus couldn't help but see the tears that were falling from her sad and liquid calf eyes. In a soft voice that belied his standing as chief among the gods of Mount Olympus Zeus asked what could possibly be troubling Io so deeply as to bring forth such great and sadtears. Io answered that for long now all that she had to eat was the dry, coarse grass at her feet. This tasteless and mean fare was hurting her mouth, rasping against her lips, and cutting into her tongue. Such a life, even when lived in the pastures of Zeus, the god of gods, had become more than she could bear. Zeus's heart was pierced with regret by these doleful words. In response he gathered up all of the tears that Io had shed and gently wiped the new ones from her long calf's eyelashes. Zeus then transformed the collected tears of Io into velvety smooth and sweet tasting wild violets. Aided by a fleecy rush of wind that sent the grasses at their feet to soft rustlings, he scattered the flowers across the surrounding fields. Thus it was that from the love and compassion of mighty Zeus for fair Io these purple, yellow and white wild violets had found their way to Malabar Farm. Even today those who know of this story, refer to wild violets as The Tears of Io.

Several hundred yards into the woods the path temporarily parallels the course of Switzer Creek as it wends its way through the forest. In this area the ground is quite damp, with skunk cabbage dominating the forest floor. I briefly left the trail to follow deer tracks down to and along the meandering edge of the creek. The water, high from spring rains, ran several feet below me, down a steep and muddy bank. Its near currents were dark and slow moving, however the opposite side of the creek was a hurried rush of water that sparkled in the sunlight as it washed over partially submerged rocks and tiny sand shoals.

The flow of Switzer Creek is in many places contained within steep, tree lined banks of mud like the one I stood looking over that day. The foundations of these walls are periodically undermined by the scouring waters of heavy downpours. In many places the overhanging banks that result from this action are being held together only by the exposed roots of the stream side trees. These trees will topple into the creek one day when the rampaging currents of spring cloudbursts cut too deeply into their base. Debris in the form of leaves, sticks, rocks, and dirt and, unfortunately, automobile tires and plastic milk jugs will begin to accumulate among the fallen trunks and branches. A dam will slowly form and Switzer Creek will begin the gradual process of carving a new channel around this obstacle. Eventually the old channel will be left behind to form another low and damp depression on the forest floor, filled with the broad leaves of skunk cabbage.

Sun dappled riffles in the water downstream indicate where Switzer Creek is shallow, flowing across exposed banks of loose pebbles. In sharp contrast are the calmer waters, like those at the base of the muddy bank below where I now paused. Here the stream runs deep, with the tangled roots of a black cherry quickly disappearing in the water's dark shadows. If I were a brook trout this is where I would hide, hidden in those shadows, waiting for some unsuspecting minnow or insect to swim or float by. A short way upstream a dogwood tree arches far over the stream, its branches heavy with white, four petaled blossoms. The countless ripples of water that flow below them shatter each blossom's reflection into myriad sparkling points of white light, each point blinking in and out of existence as the waves tear it apart, only to reform it again and again.

I was able to follow the deer trail only a short distance downstream before it turned away from the bank at a spot where the creek's edge was blocked by a maze of tattered branches from a tall maple that had fallen directly into the stream bed from the opposite side. The tree was heavy with new buds, indicating that it had fallen only recently, yet litter was already accumulating in thickening masses around branches that dragged in the water. Someday Switzer Creek will have to cut a new course around this rapidly forming obstruction. I found a notch in the bank that led me down a few muddy feet to the stream's edge and a narrow ribbon of sand and mud. Crisply etched into damp soil was the record of recent visits by a doe and her fawn, a solitary raccoon, a very busy mouse or vole, and a single bird. Climbing back up the stream bank I returned to the deer trail. It led around the fallen tree and away from the creek, then suddenly disappeared in the greening thickets of the spring forest.

Stepping over moss covered logs and across numerous dry branches and twigs, the brittle bones of last winter's ice and wind, I soon regained the Junglebrook Trail at a point where it turns away from Switzer Creek in a gradual arc to the north. Here the trail rises slightly, running for a hundred yards or more along the upper edge of a marshy, swamp-like slump where the accumulated leaves of countless years have been reduced to a rich, nearly black organic ooze. Glistening here and there in the muck are tiny pools of water, appearing like pieces of a broken mirror reflecting bits of bright blue sky and spring-green leaves. Adding additional color to this dark and boggy tableau are numerous scattered clusters of marsh marigolds. Each yellow wildflower stands out like a glowing piece of the sun against a background of dark green leaves and the even darker chocolate brown of primeval earth. Along this section of the trail, forming something of an irregular boundary between trail and bog, are several fallen trees. They lay roughly parallel to the trail, sleeping snugly in beds of fern, ground pine, and wild violets. The largest of these logs is over two feet in diameter. These massive logs, most likely victims of age and wind, have been laying here decomposing for decades and have become spongy and heavily bearded with green mosses and buff colored fungus. Deep within the creases of their brown and rotting surfaces grow tiny pearl-like mushrooms. I have heard the argument that these trees, if allowed to rot where they fall, become just so much "wasted board feet," having lost any economic value they that once held. This view is not only wrong, but is also myopically anthropocentric.

Dead trees, allowed to remain where they have fallen, provide worth in many ways far beyond their value in board feet and dollars. In the natural process of decomposition wood becomes spongy, soaking up great volumes of water during rainy seasons, and releasing it slowly during dry periods, thus keeping the forest floor relatively moist and capable of supporting new growth. Dead trees also provide crucial shelter for countless forest creatures, from the smallest insects to the black bear who finds refuge alongside or beneath them during long months of winter slumber. Last, but perhaps most important from a partisan human standpoint, these dead and decaying trees return valuable nutrients to the earth, ensuring a healthy ecosystem for future tree growth. As far as I know there have been no serious studies done examining the long-range quality of forest soils subsequent to heavy logging and clear-cutting. I wonder at the negative impact on the land of the repeated removal of such large quantities of bio-mass.

In many areas forests are now in their 3rd or 4th thirty to fifty year cycle of logging. With each new cycle the quality of the trees harvested seems to decline. Is it any wonder that the few remaining stands of unprotected virgin forests are eyed so covetously by the timber industry? Removing that much organic matter from the environment has to have a cumulative negative impact on the health of any forest ecosystem. This is a hidden cost that has rarely been factored into the economics of lumber production. Historically the timber industry has cleared the land of its forests and moved on, leaving in its wake impoverished communities hard pressed to deal with the consequences of ravaged landscapes, high unemployment, soil erosion, loss of bio-diversity, and a generally diminished environment. Louis Bromfield, in protecting and expanding the woodlands of Malabar Farm in the 1940s, was on the leading edge of a nascent forest conservation movement. Bromfield believed that a healthy human environment required not only pastures and cultivated fields, but also wild land. I imagine that he would have agreed with Henry David Thoreau's words, "In wildness is the preservation of man." Hopefully when you look upon these fallen and decaying trees you will see them, not as so much lost revenue, but rather as indispensable components of a thriving forest ecosystem. The title of an eco-folk song by Chris Brohawn and Chris Brown sums it up quite nicely *"Trees Like to Rot in the Forest."* Let these fallen giants, these old friends, rest in peace, doing what comes naturally to them.

Where the trail curves to the north to cross the wetland that inspired Louis Bromfield to give the area its "Jungle" name I passed through a sizable patch of large-flowered trillium. A scattering of common buttercups were mixed in to add an accent of yellow to the white of the trillium. I have hiked some spring woodlands where trillium has spread widely over the forest floor like a great green tapestry beaded with countless snowflakes, but not here, not in this woodland. Here the trillium was a pleasant surprise, a visual delight that was made all the more enjoyable by the flower's absence up to this point on the trail. Why trillium appears here and not elsewhere along the trail I can't say. I should also note that in my opinion there is nothing common about the common buttercup. Its diminutive and unassuming yellow petals, hiding somewhat bashfully among the previous year's fallen leaves and the spring greens of a new year, are always a pleasant addition to the painter's palette of colors that reveal themselves in the flora of an eastern hardwood forest in April and May.

In this same area I discovered one of my wife's favorite spring wildflowers, jack-in-the-pulpit. This flower looks nothing like the majority of the wildflowers that adorn the floors of our forests. A modified and stripped leaf called a spathe, beginning as a long graceful vase shape, opens up at its top then curls forward to form a pointed monk's hood over a blunted, finger-like spike that bears the plant's tiny flower. Capable of reaching three feet in height, most varieties of this plant that I have observed were under ten inches in their flowering stage. The tallest jack-in-the pulpit I have ever recorded at Malabar Farm was fourteen inches high. The spathe, along with the flower sheltered within it, begins to wither and disappear within a month or so, leaving only three large leaves drooping at the ends of firm stems. By late summer bright red and fleshy berries appear near the base of the plant, these berries are eaten by a variety of animals. This wildflower gets its name from early pioneers, who said it reminded them of a preacher in a pulpit. I prefer an even earlier and more evocative folk name for it, "The Devil's Ear", derived no doubt from its unique curving and pointed spathe and the fact that the stem, if eaten, causes a severe burning sensation in the mouth that can even result in blistering.

Just beyond the patch of trillium and the jack-in-the pulpits the trail reaches the far side of the loop and begins to make its way back to the farm lane and civilization. Here a short boardwalk leads one into and across the wetland. As wetlands go this is not a great and impressive one. There are no vast expanses of marshy water, no shallow ponds sheltering fish, no frogs or turtles. What is here is an abundance of perennially damp and muddy ground, habitat for a variety of birds including countless sparrows, red-winged blackbirds, and the shimmering swallows that swoop in from nearby fields to dine on insects. On an earlier walk here I had observed a solo marsh hawk gliding low above the abundant cattails, death on the wing for any rodent careless enough to expose itself at the wrong time. The omnipresent scribble of runic impressions in the mud along the edge of the boardwalk record the nocturnal comings and goings of raccoons, weasels, and the whitetail deer that wander freely throughout Malabar Farm's woodlands (and corn fields, to the great dismay of farm staff). Cattails are the most common plant here. On this spring day the rigid, dry and spiky stalks of last year's cattails still stood a lonely and unmoving vigil, marking the end of a long and gray winter.

Cattails are a key plant in changing wet soil into dry land. Their presence here is an early indication that this portion of the wetland is in gradual transition. Cattails produce a thick mat of horizontal root-stocks that trap masses of decaying material. As this organic debris breaks down soil is slowly formed. Eventually both the cattails and the wetland will give way to meadow and forest succession. First to come will be grasses and shrubs. They will take root in the wetland's slowly drying interior, then trees will begin to creep in from the edges. In his non-fiction books Louis Bromfield often referred to this area as a jungle, implying by those words a somewhat impenetrable environment, but on this walk, as with others taken in different seasons, it didn't come across as intimidating.

I suspect that this ground is already much dryer than it was in Bromfield's time. Perhaps in a few more decades this portion of Malabar's wetland will disappear into the surrounding forest. However, somewhere nearby, possibly in the wildness systematically reclaiming the forgotten fields of an abandoned farm in an neighboring valley, there will be a fractured and fragmented subterranean sandstone block that will slowly crumble, forming a slump. Rain water will gradually collect in this depression. The water will filter down through the sandstone until it reaches deeper layers of impermeable clay, then a shallow pond will form and life will gradually enter it. The eggs of fish and frogs will arrive on the feet and feathers of passing waterfowl. Turtles will somehow manage to find their way to the new pond. Pond lilies will blanket the water's surface with their mottled green leaves and white petaled flowers. Mice will come to investigate along the water's edge. Barred and great horned owls will come to dine on the mice. All of this will be overseen by deer who quench their thirst in the heat of summer. In the decades that follow organic matter from dying weeds, water lilies, and a million fallen leaves will combine with the decomposing bodies of countless pond animals to settle on the muddy floor of the pond. Over many more years this detritus will silently and patiently accumulate. Inch by methodical inch a nutrient rich organic sediment will form. The pond's floor will rise, cattails and sedges will appear along its shore. The cattails will begin their inexorable advance inward and the pond's circumference will slowly decrease, until the pond finally disappears. Still, in the death of the pond a new wetland of rich and oozing black soil will be born. Transition and evolution are the way of all things, whether we approve or not.

Beyond the cattails and the wetland the Junglebrook Trail ascends a gentle slope to enter a narrow strip of upland woods. Here, sandwiched between the wetland and a farm field, grow beech, maple, black cherry, red oak, and a scattering of hickory and flowering dogwoods. The trees along the upper edge of the hillside are silhouetted against the high plane of the field, backed by a broad sky. This early in the year the farm field remains bare, the soil held together by moisture and the remnants of last season's soybeans. I have been told that this year the crop will be corn. Louis Bromfield practiced a system of crop rotation that typically included corn, oats and wheat, and sometimes a fallow year. This particular field, the northern boundary of the Jungle, became Louis Bromfield's truck garden, eight acres dedicated to growing the vegetables that were sold at his produce stand located near the old Schrack house, today's Malabar Farm Restaurant. Bromfield wrote that these acres produced the most income per acre of any land at Malabar Farm.

The trail along the wooded hillside follows a line parallel to and twenty to forty feet above the wetland. At first it is cattails that fill the low ground, only grudgingly do they give way to isolated clusters of dark green skunk cabbage. Gradually the skunk cabbage begins to dominate the water soaked soil. Thriving in the black and glistening ooze, the skunk cabbage covers the western end of the wetland in a thick, shag-like carpet of lush greens. For the time being this part of Bromfield's Jungle remains very much a "wet" land.

137

A few scattered trillium struggle to grow along this hillside and wild violets appear in abundance among the grasses that bracket the trail, but for the most part wildflowers don't seem to care much for this dryer forest environment. On previous walks along this hillside the forest floor has been buried beneath inches of snow or covered with thick summer vegetation. This time, however, I was able to see something I had never noticed before. With the forest floor still relatively free of new growth, a glint of sunlight reflecting off a fragment of glass caught my attention. At first I thought it was a single broken bottle, something thoughtlessly discarded by an earlier hiker, but in scrambling up the hill to retrieve the pieces, I discovered that the ground was littered not only with the broken glass of both bottles and jars, but also with assorted pieces of rusting metal and small shards of shattered pottery. A trash dump of sorts was spilling down the hillside from the field above.

Trash dumps have often been treasure troves of information for archeologists studying early cultures and civilizations, but in examining the objects at this site I quickly decided that nothing here appeared to be older than perhaps five or six decades. I didn't, however, find any aluminum cans or plastic material, candy wrappers and such, which would indicate that this site had been active in recent years. Nonetheless in the not too distant past someone had decided that this would be a great place to dispose of their rubbish. Moreover, enough debris had accumulated here to suggest that dumping had happened more than once. Between 1957 and 1972 the Louis Bromfield Malabar Farm Foundation operated the farm. I suspect that this trash was from those years, perhaps a "dirty little secret" for the otherwise environmentally conscious Foundation members. I couldn't help pondering over the question of how many additional generations it would take before this junk pile would be transformed into some scholar's collection of historic artifacts.

Allowing my imagination to run free for a few moments I began to speculate on what older treasures might be buried beneath this pile of modern trash, treasures now concealed below the pickle jars, rusting steel cans, and broken ceramics of the recent past. Perhaps belt buckles, square nails, bone buttons, or even the hammer of a shattered flintlock lay hidden here. Might it be possible that these pioneer artifacts hid even more ancient secrets, an arrowhead or two, fragments of coiled clay pots, a roughly sculpted mortar stone... or even the rounded and grooved stone of a war club? I doubted that this would be the case, but then again someone had recently chosen this particular location to rid themselves of their accumulated trash. Might they simply have been following the lead of an earlier people?

Cleaning up this modern trash dump would be a good project for Park volunteers. Then maybe we could have a look at what lies hidden beneath. Having said this I must admit that I have learned from experience that there are times when it is better to leave things to one's imagination. I came to this understanding years ago on the narrow country roads that led to my mother-in-law's home in northeast Ohio. On these trips I would pass what appeared to be a little used township road, a narrow macadam lane that began in a dark tunnel of green trees. This road was barely wide enough for two vehicles to pass each other, thus allowing the tunnel of trees to work like a lens that focused one's attention on a distant yellow circle and the hazy and sunlit world beyond. I imagined this world to be filled with whitewashed farmhouses and great red barns topped by high cupolas. I imagined brightly colored quilts drying on clotheslines, and dark brown earth being tilled by sun burnt men wearing broad brimmed straw hats, straining to keep powerful Belgians or Percherons in check. This, I knew, was the bucolic, lilac scented world of Shirley Temple in *Rebecca of Sunnybrook Farm,* my favorite of the many Shirley Temple films that my wife loves so much.

After resisting the temptation for years I finally decided to turn down that narrow blacktop lane to see what was there, to enter that pastoral world that I had envisioned so often and in such detail. I should have left it all to my imagination, I should have resisted the urge to explore that particular road, I should have left it a road not taken, but I didn't, and on that day my world diminished just a little bit. I found no enormous Belgians, powerful muscles straining to pull sharp plows through open fields, I saw no log-cabin quilts draped across the railings of inviting front porches, there were no sun bonneted women tending flower beds or bending over vegetable gardens, there were no men shaded from the sun under broad brimmed straw hats.

My wonderful Arcadian landscape evaporated in a world of modern ranch homes, television antennas, pick-up trucks, riding lawnmowers, and above-ground swimming pools. Barely visible at the edge of this miscellany of 21th century life lay the sad and graying remnants of abandoned and long neglected barns. These forlorn structures were ending their days obscured behind the countless volunteer trees that had sprouted along their sides, trees whose branches were insinuating themselves into and splintering hundred year old boards, trees whose roots were snaking into the cracks of massive sandstone blocks, undermining the very foundations of these ancient buildings. In 1955 artist and author Eric Slone penned a book about this very subject. The title he gave his book sums it up quite well, *Our Vanishing Landscape.*

Beyond the trash strewn hillside and near the trail's end the path slowly descends to the upper reaches of the wetland. There used to be a boardwalk here that led through boggy ground covered with skunk cabbage.[16] Skunk cabbage actually produces a wildflower, by far the most unusual wildflower that Malabar Farm has to offer. This plant's flower is so strange that many people don't even realize that skunk cabbage is a flowering plant.

Skunk cabbage is a true harbinger of spring, forcing its way through the muck of swamps and muddy lowlands on balmy late winter days. As though anticipating the need for an early start, this plant begins its development in the fall so that it is ready to bloom at the first hint of sustained warmth. Heat generated by cellular activity at this emergent stage of the skunk cabbage's development can raise the ground temperature around the plant by as much as twenty degrees, often melting any snow that is there. As its tightly curled and horn-shaped hood pushes upward through the damp earth it begins to unfurl, releasing a foul aroma that permeates the cold air. This repellent odor and the large cabbage like leaves that develop later give the plant its name. Sheltered within the tightly wrapped hood, to be revealed only as it opens, grows the flower. This flower isn't the brightly colored wildflower so commonly associated with spring but is instead a delicate, flesh colored "bloom," attached to the end of a finger-like stalk. Even the skunk cabbage's method of pollination seems to argue against its recognition as the earliest of spring wildflowers. The skunk cabbage is pollinated by small carrion flies attracted to the plant by its odor of decaying flesh.

My hike along The Junglebrook Trail ended where the mud and skunk cabbage ends, at a grassy area alongside Malabar's farm lane only a few yards from where the walk had started. Now approaching the noon hour, it was time to enjoy a retracing of my steps back along the dirt road, back past the stubbly brown fields that awaited the corn and soybeans that would soon blanket them, back past the picket fence that enclosed the ancient cemetery, back past grass covered fields and along green pastures, their distant reaches dotted with curious calves and their more docile mothers. I ambled on, and being in no particular hurry imagined that I was walking alongside Louis Bromfield as he strolled this same lane seventy years ago the stubbly grass that ran down its middle brushing against his ankles. I could see him kicking up dust as he leaned against a fence post

Malabar Farm, c1945   photograph courtesy Malabar Farm State Park

to watch his grazing herd of Holsteins.[17] I could see him turning slowly to smile with satisfaction as he studied his undulating fields of slowly greening grass. In the distance was his Big House. Nestled serenely upon a low hillside that backed up to a dark sandstone cliff, the house glowed invitingly in the yellow-white of a mid-day sun. The image that played before my mind's eye may not have been the richly colored and pastoral Sunnybrook Farm of my imagination... but it was pretty close.

## Chapter 5

# A Log Cabin, A Rocky Place, and A Wall of Ice

In the mid 1930s, shortly before Louis Bromfield started buying the land in Pleasant Valley to create Malabar Farm, James Pugh, an employee of Ohio Power (later to become Ohio Edison), purchased several acres of land on a wooded hillside that was accessed by the old Ferguson/Newville Road. In the years that followed this land would be completely surrounded by Malabar Farm. In 1938 Pugh, using old electric poles, built a weekend retreat cabin in his woods. Pugh was a resourceful man placing

The Pugh Cabin, Malabar Farm State Park.

his logs for his cabin by using an ingenious system of ropes, cables, and pulleys strung from surrounding trees. The cabin was built on a base of sandstone blocks that came from the foundations of the recently abandoned town of Newville. Newville stones, cut and shaped by James Pugh's hand, were also used to make a patio and the low landscaping walls around his

143

cabin. He also used the stone to create a pair of entrance pillars at the approach to his cabin.

Pugh built a spring fed pond behind his cabin. He then added a small deck that extended a dozen feet into the pond. Using additional Newville foundation stones, also cut and shaped by his own hand, Pugh built a low wall to enclose a small sand covered beach. A few years later a picnic shelter was added on a gentle rise a few yards behind his cabin. A huge sandstone boulder sat where the shelter was to be built. The boulder was far too large to move, so Pugh planned to dynamite the rock, breaking it into more manageable pieces. While digging beneath the stone to place dynamite he uncovered the remains of what he could only imagine was a long dead Indian. Examination by a local doctor confirmed that the bones were human and very old. Choosing not to disturb the site of what was almost certainly an ancient grave, Pugh decided to incorporate the boulder into the northern end of his shelter. He built a fireplace in the southern wall and later added side walls to enclose the structure.

The Pugh picnic shelter with the massive boulder wall.

In 1956 Pugh constructed another cabin and pond a

hundred yards from his first one. It was also built of old telephone poles from Ohio Power. Additional foundation stones from Newville were used for a fireplace and chimney. Both cabins survive. This second cabin includes a beautiful deck that faces out onto the pond. In early summer this pond is blanketed with deep green lily pads, most of them adorned with white blossoms, their huge petals curving outward to reveal bright yellow stamens. With a blue and cloudless sky overhead to reflect in the dark waters surrounding the lily pads, and with a slight breeze to stir the water and set the pads to rocking in gentle undulations, you might imagine that you have been transported back to 1899 and Claude Monet's French garden and lily pond at Giverney. You might even be able to envision that bearded and aging gentleman sitting at his easel, capturing on his canvas the beauty of the sun, and sky, the water, and the lilies. This second Pugh cabin now sits empty. It was, however, occupied by a young Park employee until a few years ago. He married and his new wife didn't want to live in a cabin in the woods with a porch that overlooked a lily filled pond. So the cabin was abandoned. This move is something I don't understand. What more idyllic location for a newlywed couple could one possibly imagine? I have often wondered how that marriage has fared.

When Jim Pugh retired, he and his wife Georgia made the original 1938 cabin their full time retirement home. The Pughs became friends of Louis Bromfield, probably a good thing since his land completely encircled their few acres, except for access to the cabins on the old Ferguson Road. In 1972, sixteen years after Bromfield's death, the State of Ohio acquired Malabar Farm. In 1976 Malabar Farm became a State Park. Jim Pugh had died in 1974, and soon afterward the State of Ohio forced Georgia Pugh to sell the Pugh home and wooded acres that went with it. The Pugh family believed the "fair market value" of $120,000 was too low, but Georgia agreed to the price and moved to Mansfield, where she died in 1989. Although the landscaping walls that enclose the 1938 cabin have been neglected and the little dock has collapsed into the pond, both Pugh cabins have been maintained by the Park and are used for various Park activities. The original cabin is also rented to the public for day use purposes.

What would Louis Bromfield, who by his nature was a very generous person, have thought about how the State treated, or dare I say "bullied" Georgia Pugh. In the 1930's, when the Federal Government took land in the Smoky Mountains to create The Great Smoky Mountain National Park, they found themselves confronted by individuals who didn't want to sell. Eventually the government came to an agreement with these people that allowed them to remain in their homes for the remainder of their lifetimes if they so desired. Only after they died would their property be absorbed into the National Park. It was sixty years before the last of these properties finally became part of the Great Smoky Mountain National Park. It seems that the State of Ohio could have made the same compassionate arrangement with Georgia Pugh. What was the hurry? At most the State would have had to wait a decade or two, and an aging widow wouldn't have been evicted from the home that her husband had built thirty-nine years earlier using his own hands and ingenuity.

Malabar Farm's Butternut Trail starts at the 1938 Pugh Cabin. The trail's beginning is clearly marked where it enters a small grove of hemlocks just beyond the cabin. This is a lollypop trail, meaning that it goes into the woods for about a quarter of a mile before it reaches a Y. At that point the trail becomes a loop of another three-quarters of a mile. The approach to the Y leads gradually up hill, paralleling a narrow ravine on the right. A high rugged cliff of dark sandstone rises dramatically out of the upper end of this ravine. From May through October this rocky monolith is somewhat obscured, first behind the lush green leaves of spring and summer, then in autumn behind a blaze of yellow, orange and scarlet.

The surface of this sandstone cliff, the projecting face of a massive outcropping, is deeply scored with the black lines of countless cracks and fissures. A short and well defined path leads down to the cliff's boulder strewn base. From its base the sandstone rises dramatically out of the depths of the ravine, reaching upward some thirty feet to a grass covered top. A yawning vertical cavity, the largest of the outcropping's many cracks, splits the wall. This great crack in the sandstone is known as the Malabar Farm "Cave." On seeing it for the first time it becomes obvious why it has acquired this name. A short scramble across roots and boulders finds you standing before a gaping black triangular mouth, about ten feet wide at its muddy and debris cluttered floor. Rough, sandpaper-like walls slope gradually inward until the crack closes a dozen or more feet overhead. The erosion patterns on the stony floor at your feet give evidence of the ages it must have taken to form the deep ravine that runs below the crevice's opening. Cloudbursts still send water wending through this crack. In the summer the entrance to this opening is tightly framed by green ferns and small trees. The outer reaches of the crevice's moist surfaces, those spots where sun manages to briefly touch, are clothed in the soft textures of thick and spongy mosses.

I chose mid-summer for the walk described here because for this book's purposes I wanted to experience Malabar in all its seasons and I had not as yet touched on summer. Thus, on a sun filled, blue sky morning in early July I found myself standing at the entrance to the cave.[18] Upon entering this deep crevice I was quickly enveloped in a dark, damp, and I have to say, very cave-like environment. The rapid transition from the green and organic sunlit world of an Ohio hardwood forest to the hard, abrasive and chilled world of sandstone and night was jolting. I moved slowly forward into the cool darkness, picking my way carefully across a floor of seeping mud and shallow pools of black water. The passage gradually narrowed and the way grew dimmer. The bright sunlight that had spotlighted the cave's entrance offered less and less illumination.

As I pressed inward the passage quickly transitioned into an inky and furtive blackness. Eyes were of little help now as I moved forward in near total blackness. Touch took over as my primary sense as I cautiously eased myself up and over a large boulder. Hands scraped tentatively along the rough surface of sandstone walls until I came to a point where the passage abruptly turned to the left. Here the walls of the cave pressed inward, narrowing the passageway to the point where I had to turn sideways to continue. In the darkness my hands traced protrusions and indentations in the walls. One side mirrored the other, a bulge in the rock on my left neatly mirroring a depression in the rock on my right. I found myself moving through what was becoming less and less a cave and more and more a very deep cleaving of a very large rock.

Exiting Malabar Farm's "Cave"

The floor of the cave rose slowly as I inched along the narrow crack, stumbling here and there over hidden rocks. At one point I found it necessary to lean forward at the waist to pass through an especially tight squeeze where an angled shelf of the

148

gritty stone made standing upright impossible. Although still enveloped in deep shadow, looking up I could now see a thin, jagged slice of blue sky, tree branches and the silhouettes of arcing ferns suspended some twenty to twenty-five feet above me. Little more was needed to confirm that this was in fact a crevice and not a true cave. As the crack widened, sunlight began to find its way deeper into the rock and the way forward became much easier to see. Looking overhead I could see the rounded bottom of a huge and ominous looking boulder. Somehow, in ages long past, this giant, egg shaped rock had become wedged into the upper reaches of this crack. It now hung there, suspended between the two worlds of sunlight and shadow. As I made my way forward the crevice expanded, terminating in a rocky climb to the forest floor and the glare of bright sunlight and green trees. Following a somewhat daunting hand by foot scramble over assorted boulders that littered the way I emerged into daylight, finding myself standing on the roof of the massive sandstone outcropping that held Malabar's cave, its dark entrance now far below me.

Louis Bromfield, writing in *Pleasant Valley* in 1945, told of digging in the vicinity of the cave and unearthing what appeared to be a carefully prepared burial site for six Indians. Their bodies had been placed side by side upon a bed of gravel, apparently used to drain the mass grave. He further speculated that these unfortunate individuals might have been killed in a long forgotten battle. One skeleton had a crushed skull and another a broken and shattered shoulder and arm. The bodies were carefully reburied by Bromfield and I can only assume that, like the body beneath Jim Pugh's boulder, they remain there today. Unfortunately no visible evidence of Bromfield's excavations survives, and his description of the dig's location is vague, so exactly where these six warrior's rest is a mystery, and perhaps it is better that way.

It enriches one's experience of this land to realize that as you walk the valleys and wooded hillsides of Malabar Farm you are doing so in the footsteps of invisible companions from years long past. In some places you are literally walking upon ground rendered sacred by the burials of long forgotten individuals, people who lived and hunted, perhaps even fought and died in these woods. In their essential natures they were a people not all that much different from us. Like us they must have loved, raised children, defended their homes, and surely they had their dreams. No doubt they also had disappointments, hopefully these were tempered by times of joy. If their burials are any evidence, Bromfield's unnamed Indians also had companions who honored and cared for them, friends and family who mourned their passing. Now only their bones remain, slowly becoming part of the soil in the woodlands of Malabar Farm.

The high roof of the sandstone monolith that holds the cave is crowned by a flat expanse of rock that has been softened by a thin blanket of leafy soil. This earthen covering, no more than a few inches in depth, is the product of countless leaves, falling season after season for hundreds, if not thousands of years. It now supports thick grasses, some ferns, and even a few small trees. These trees may, however, have overreached, and their lives most likely will be brief. The hulks of several recently fallen trees currently litter the area, looking like the disorderly confusion of thin slivers from a giant game of Pick-Up-Sticks. The failed efforts of earlier trees are also visible, their crumbling trunks, now fungus and moss covered, contribute nutrients to the duff of a patiently developing forest floor. Although at first glance it isn't recognizable as such, an exploration of the surrounding area soon reveals that you are in fact standing on a thin layer of soil covering hard rock. The most immediate and obvious evidence for this is an ominous black line that slices through the textured surface of leaves and grass at your feet. By inching cautiously up to it and leaning slightly forward you will find yourself gazing into the void of a narrow and very deep chasm. When I did this a brief wave of vertigo passed through me, settling in my stomach as the blackness seemed to be drawing me into it.

Backing away from the edge I dropped to my hands and knees and once again crept tentatively up to the menacing crack. Peering into it for a second time I could see ragged stone walls dropping away far below me. Although illuminated near the surface by angled shafts of sunlight, these walls quickly disappeared into a breathtaking darkness. This "ominous black line" is the gaping top of the great crevice that I had so recently passed through. It cuts a zig-zag path across the grass for some thirty to forty feet. At no point is it more than three or four feet wide. A careless slip here could easily result in a plunge of some twenty feet or more, bouncing from side to side against hard, unforgiving sandstone, and ending very badly with a muffled thud in the darkness far below.

Scientists aren't sure when or how this huge crevice and its smaller companions were formed in the sandstone, but a plausible theory is that they are the result of thousands of years and countless expansions and contractions of ice wedges in minute cracks in the rock during pre-glacial or inter-glacial periods. The last glacial period, named the Wisconsin Glacial Episode because it was first studied in that state, ended about 10,000 to 12,500 years ago. This glacier was only the latest in a long series of glacial periods and the ice ages that produced them. The Wisconsin Ice Sheet began to form far north in Canada some 70,000 years ago, but it didn't reach Ohio for another 50,000 years. These dates can be considered fairly accurate because of the carbon 14 dating of significant quantities of organic material, bones, shells, and wood that remain in glacial deposits today.

A detailed glacial map, produced by the Geological Survey Division of the Ohio Department of Natural Resources, illustrates the extent of all known glaciation periods across Ohio. The map describes a series of irregular end moraines, the leading edge of glaciers, which spread diagonally across the state from the northeast to the southwest. Even a brief glance at this map

151

shows that during some part of these many glaciations nearly two-thirds of Ohio lay buried beneath a thick sheet of ice. The map also shows that 200,000 years ago the Illinoian glacier pushed far south of present day Richland County. During the later Wisconsin glaciation, however, there was a finger of ice free land that extended into what is now the southeastern portion of the county. This land was bordered on the north, west, and southwest by a massive wall of ice. Perhaps a half mile thick at its edge, this wall would have been visible from any high open ground. Located within that glacier free finger of land were the rolling hills and wide valleys that thousands of years later would become famous as Louis Bromfield's Malabar Farm.

The sandstone outcropping and its popular cave are the furthest that most people investigate on the Butternut Trail. The path to the cave is wide and in many places overlaid with a latticework of thick tree roots. Crawling across soil that has been compacted by the weight of countless shoes, these roots have become darkened and hardened with age and exposure. Heavy foot traffic has also burnished their gnarled surfaces to a satiny finish. Thus transformed, the roots now resemble huge and wonderfully textured snakes, frozen in place, patiently waiting to trip the careless walker and send him or her sprawling onto the hard packed earth.

At a point on the trail near the cave, on a slight rise approximately parallel to the cave's entrance, sits a huge maple tree. Growing out of the earth and moss that surrounds the roots of this tree is a rare plant, the only example of a walking fern (*Asplenium rhizophyllum*) known to exist in Richland County. The walking fern is an interesting plant. With fronds half an inch wide and at most only two or three inches in length, the fern derives its name from the way it extends these pointed fronds outward until they droop to contact a surface, where an attempt is made to take root. If successful the fern will continue to grow, sending out additional fronds that droop and hopefully find fertile ground for continued development. In this way it slowly "walks" away from its original rooting. For as long as I have been aware of this rare and diminutive fern it has led a precarious life at Malabar Farm. Year after year it struggles vainly to climb the thickly indented and mossy bark of the tree, unaware of the ultimate futility of its efforts in this direction. Some years it manages to extend itself upward a foot or two, at other times it barely clings to life a few inches above the earth. Never has it looked especially healthy, but then it is the only walking fern I have ever seen, so I'm not sure what a healthy one is supposed to look like.

Exiting the cave I resumed my hike, ascending the trail that continued beyond the cave's grassy and crevice fractured roof. Minutes later I innocently blundered into what must have been a private chipmunk confab, my uninvited appearance apparently resulting in a serious disturbance to the assemblage's deliberations. I was immediately assaulted on all sides by the chiding voices of no less that seven different chipmunks. Several of these fellows, black and white racing stripes streaking their tan flanks, stood upon fallen logs, quivering in outrage. Two emerged to scold me from hiding places in the deeply segmented crevices of a nearby sandstone block. Another's beady black eyes stared accusingly at me from a dark hole beneath the block. One poked a pointed and obviously quite agitated nose out from a small tunnel concealed beneath rust colored leaves heaped against the gray and moldering edge of a fallen beech. With sharp, indignant and rapid-fire chattering all seven let me know in no uncertain terms that I was an unwelcome intruder. Bouncing all about me in a blur of jerky starts and stops, these tiny balls of frantic fur leaped agilely from the gray surfaces of surrounding rocks to the leaf and fern blanketed forest floor, from forest floor to the moss covered bark of nearby logs, from the logs back the rocks and forest floor, all the while continuing their incensed harangue. Finally, having apparently sated their wrath, they finished their rant with one final piercing chorus of angry chirps, then vanished into hidden passageways, disappearing as quickly as they had appeared. In all of this staccato scolding not one fellow paused long enough for me to take his portrait.

Beyond the cave the trail narrows considerably, being much less traveled than the well beaten section of the trail that leads up to it. A few hundred feet beyond the exit of the cave is the Y that marks the beginning of the loop section of the trail. The loop itself possesses no particularly outstanding landscape or geologic features. For the most part it is simply a pleasant if uninspiring stroll through a young woodland. It does, nonetheless, have the advantage of being an excellent place for solitude, as relatively few people venture beyond the cave. Here one's attention can be directed to the little things, and on this particular hike those little things stood out in abundance. As I wrote in the previous chapter, artist Georgia O'Keeffe wanted people to notice the little things. She wanted them to appreciate the smaller details of nature that are usually overlooked in the rush of our modern technologically driven lives. Some of her close-up images of the organically sensual interiors of flowers have been interpreted as being overtly erotic. She denied such an intent. Perhaps her emphasis on observation and attention to detail was her way of deflecting the sexually charged opinions of those critics. In response to one interviewer's question concerning this issue she turned the tables on the critics, saying that any impression of eroticism must have been generated in the critic's own mind and thoughts. Regardless of her true intentions, Georgia O'Keeffe has always been among my favorite artists, and so this day was to be a day given over to slowing down, to pausing to observe things more closely, a day for not merely looking at, but for really observing "the little things."

Turning right at the Y my attention was soon drawn to a partially uprooted sugar maple. Leaning at an acute angle away from the trail it appeared frozen in mid fall. The roots, violently torn from the earth, tilted upward like an inverted saucer, several feet above the forest floor. A few roots, hanging downward like a spider's legs, still clung to the ground. A subterranean world of primal rock and earth lay exposed in the shadowy hollow beneath the elevated tangle of dirt and roots. This great tree, its base no less than two feet in diameter, had seemingly been thrown over by high winds during one of several severe storms that had pummeled Malabar Farm in the recent past. Before crashing to the ground, the massive trunk of this tree managed to lodge itself against another tree, a tree obviously better anchored to the soil than the maple had been. Here the tree remained, terminally injured, but still standing with the support of another, caught between the sky and the earth, looking very much like an abandoned column thrown over in the ruins of an ancient Greek temple.

Closing my eyes I could envision the dramatic tempest that has broken this great tree. A warm and tranquil late summer afternoon is suddenly transformed into night by black clouds that rise rapidly from the west. Gathering ominously overhead, these clouds quickly churn themselves into a roiling fury. Peals of thunder are launched across the forest in ear-splitting crescendos. Lightning fractures the darkened sky with jagged streaks of yellow. A frenzied blast of wind whipsaws trees, hurling leaves, twigs, and broken branches through the air like bursts of shrapnel. Torrents of rain pound out a furious drumbeat, keeping time with the havoc of the storm. Deer flee in terror and squirrels cower in dens, their trembling heads turned inward from the mayhem. Amidst the chaos of this unchecked tumult there is a sudden deafening explosion of dirt, rocks, sticks, and leaves. The tall maple, its roots violently ripped from the soil, is thrown into an arcing curve toward the earth. A thunderous collision with the forest floor is averted only when the maple is caught in mid fall by a much better grounded oak. Moments pass, the fury of the storm abates, and a palpable quiet settles across the forest.

Most of the damaged tree's roots, having borne the full

fury of the storm, hang torn and limp in the open air. A few roots, those fortunate enough to be located along the hinge of the aborted fall, remain buried in the earth. These roots, having been spared the storm's worst, will for a time struggle to provide sufficient nutrients to keep the tree alive, if only on life-support. For a while the maple's leaves will remain green and the tree will struggle to grow. Its ultimate fate, however, has been sealed by the storm. Slowly the tree will die. In time its wood will weaken to the point where it will crack and splinter, then collapse. Perhaps it will settle gracefully to the earth, more likely it will drop in one sudden and thunderous crash. Contact with the moist earth and the microbes living there will hasten decomposition. Mother Nature is in no hurry though, and this may take many decades. In this way the soil will be enriched, generating fertile ground for a new generation of maples.

Only yards beyond the dying maple I found a textbook example of just such a process of decay and renewal. Barely visible, nearly lost in a blanket of leaves, grasses, and ferns on the forest floor, is the barely recognizable trunk of a tree. Only a slender and crumbling thread of rust colored wood, the rotting corpse of the tree, remains. It won't be long before even this will completely dissolve into the black earth that is patiently absorbing it. The nutrients still retained by this long dead tree are now being released at an accelerating pace. Perhaps they will nourish a nearby sapling that will in its turn become a giant of the forest. Like its long dead ancestor, our newly broken maple will one day return to the earth, and the sustaining cycle of birth-death-rebirth will continue as it has for countless ages.

Louis Bromfield, writing in *Out Of The Earth* (1950), had the following to say with reference to man's relationship to the earth that sustains him:

*"But most of all there is the earth and the animals through which one comes very close to eternity and the secrets of the universe."*

Biographer Ivan Scott, at the conclusion of *Louis Bromfield, Novelist and Agrarian Reformer* (1991), summed up his subject's life and connection to the soil by noting that it is while exploring the hills and valleys, and the fields and forests of Malabar Farm that one is most likely to encounter the living spirit of Louis Bromfield.

Beyond the uprooted maple the landscape rises slowly but steadily, with only occasional dips here and there imitating the broad swells of a calm sea. The trees, among them maple, striped maple, ash, a scattering of black cherry, some sassafras, and yes, butternut, are relatively small, most of them probably not more than fifty to seventy-five years old, suggesting that this woodland was an open field not too many years before Malabar Farm was started. Sometime shortly before or soon after Louis Bromfield purchased this land in 1939[19] an aerial photograph of the Herring property and the surrounding countryside was taken. Perhaps Bromfield himself had the photograph taken, as the Herring farmhouse, the future site of his Big House, sits near the middle of the composition. A small portion of the hillside below the cave is visible in the upper left of that photograph. Although wooded, it appears to have been relatively open, almost park like, with the trees separated from one another by considerable expanses of bare ground. From the photograph it is hard to determine the heights of the trees, but most of them do not appear to be very tall. In *Pleasant Valley* (1945) Bromfield wrote that before he purchased this land, livestock had been turned loose to graze across the wooded hills. Cattle and pigs had so completely denuded the ground of growing things, including saplings, that the forest had no chance of regenerating naturally. One of Bromfield's first jobs on his new farm was to remove the livestock from the woods and enclose the woodlands within fences. This would give the forest an opportunity to renew itself naturally, a process that could take decades. Remnants of his fence posts and barbed wire can still be found in many places along the fringes of Malabar's woodland acres. After Bromfield's death in 1956 the Friends of the Land, followed a short time later by the Louis Bromfield Malabar Farm Foundation, assumed ownership and operation of Malabar Farm. The Foundation continued the process of renewal by planting thousands of additional trees on Malabar's hillsides.

As it nears the top of the hill The Butternut Trail circles to the east, then turns north and downhill to begin its looping return to the cave. It was here that I came across one of the largest wild grape vines I have ever seen. Considering its size I'm sure it has been here for a long time, but this was the first time I actually noticed it. Four to five inches in diameter for much of its great length, the vine twists its serpentine route languidly through the branches of several trees. Its black surface is roughly textured, the loose shreds of dry and brittle bark crumbing into a course dust when rubbed vigorously between one's fingers. Quite sensuous in its free-form growth, the vine appears to be frozen in both place and time, a shaggy fossilized python, eternally trapped in a silent pose, though straining with both tension and purpose. Seeing this giant vine brought to mind decades old memories of exploring the woods near my grandfather's farm, memories of swinging on grapevines strung from trees much like these ones.

Wild grapevines, although somewhat sinister in their snake-like appearance, can serve a vital role in survival situations. Even when wet the shredding bark of this vine can be used as an excellent tinder for starting a campfire. Of course you will still need something to spark that fire, so waterproof matches should be a part of every emergency kit. A flint and steel sparking set will work, or you might even learn how to construct your own bow-drill. However, unless you know yourself to be a modern-day Daniel Boone I would suggest a good supply of the matches. I imagine that if they had been available to him Daniel himself would have been happy to carry them. He didn't hesitate to hunt with a  rifle, although I am sure that he also knew how to use a bow and arrow.

Where the Butternut Trail turns north to complete its loop it briefly runs parallel to the Pleasant Valley Bridle Trail that encircles Malabar Farm. It was here that I decided to leave the Butternut trail and join the horse trail where it passes through the western portion of Ferguson Meadow.[20] From previous hikes I knew that the remaining section of the Butternut loop is, for the most part, a continuance of what I had already seem. I wanted to experience the contrasting environment of the high meadow, that land that Louis Bromfield described as a place of "solitude in the midst of beauty and plenty." The meadow was near enough that on this sunny day I could easily see it through the woods. Bright, sunlit grasses contrasted sharply with a shadow filled screen of silhouetted trees, producing the illusion of an exquisitely rendered India ink drawing, its multifaceted black lines sketched against a pastel background of greens and yellows.

Leaving the trail I headed for an aging black walnut tree that grows along the edge of the meadow. I think of this particular walnut as a tree of competing personalities. In the summer its forest side is perpetually cloked in deep shadows, while its meadow side indulges in the warmth of open sunlight. As I related in an earlier chapter, the black walnut is among my favorite trees. However, in giving my reasons for this I failed to mention an important one, the tree's almond shaped leaves. Paired in groupings of nine to twenty-nine leaflets, they produce a most delightful oriental pattern when silhouetted against a bright blue sky. There is, however, something else typical of black walnuts that isn't as pleasing as its leafy designs. If you have ever handled the husks of black walnuts after they have begun to decompose,

Black walnut branches and leaves silhouetted against the summer sky.

then you know that they will stain anything that comes in contact with them, hands, gloves, shirt sleeves, pant legs. Fortunately even this unpleasant characteristic has a silver lining. Long ago our pioneer ancestors used black walnut husks to make a rich, dark brown writing ink.

Passing beneath the arched branches of the black walnut I stepped into the sunlit western meadow. It still took some plodding through thick, waist-high tangles of grass, plus a brief pause to re-tie beleaguered shoelaces, before I finally reached the bridle trail. The wild diversity of this western meadow greatly surpasses the somewhat more restrained character of its sister to the east. The bridle trail passes through the entire length of the western meadow, turning south only at the remnants of the Ferguson Road that divides the two sides of the meadow. The trail through the meadow is a deeply cut dirt path, its route tightly hemmed in by walls of tall grass and weeds. Warm July breezes race freely through the field, setting grasses, weeds, and even the many purple tipped thistles that grow among them, to gentle swaying. Tight clusters of petite white flowers, common yarrow, ride like effervescent foam atop this floating sea of greens, yellows, and purples.

The western meadow is slowly shrinking. The forest seems to be gradually reclaiming its edges. Copses of shrubs and small trees have taken root within the field, forming small arboreal islands surrounded by weedy grasslands. This part of the meadow, unlike its more domesticated eastern side, is an unrestrained explosion of earthy color. I have walked this tract on sunny autumn days and found myself transfixed by trees, shrubs, weeds, and grasses adorned in such a breathtaking variety of browns, purples, reds, oranges, yellows and white as to be almost beyond imagining. Even in the mellow heat of this typical mid-summer day the western meadow was incandescent in the bright sunlight, offering a rich palette of green and golden brown hues, stippled with white and purple and set against the dark wall of the forest. As I emerged from the somber shadows of the surrounding woods, the visual contrast between forest and field was immediate and intense. No artist could have done better than nature herself in creating the powerfully evocative scenery that opened invitingly before me.

Standing motionless on the trail the first thing I noticed was the quiet and the stillness. Only the grasses and the wildflowers were moving, urged into rippling undulations by elusive breezes. It was only when I began to move down the trail that the meadow truly came alive with activity and motion. Suddenly I found myself surrounded with life and movement. A black swallowtail butterfly rose from the yellow petals of a nearby ox-eye daisy. Flying grasshoppers, rising and falling in choppy starts and stops, danced along the dusty trail ahead of my feet. Loud buzzing alerted me to a nervous bumblebee, my unexpected appearance apparently having disturbed him in his meanderings among the blossoms of red clover that thrive in the grasses along the narrow edges of the trail. A green and blue dragonfly hung suspended overhead like a toy helicopter. It paused for a few moments, then raced away in sudden pursuit of some unknown objective. Several more butterflies, tiny yellow specimens with wings no bigger than my thumbnail, flitted about in pairs, fluttering from scattered milkweed stalks to the golden stamens of daisies, from daisies to nearby yarrow, from yarrow back to daisies, never resting for more than a second or two, impossible to photograph.

Also thriving within this smorgasbord of color and motion is my nemesis, poison ivy. It appears in intermittent patches along the sunlit borders of the trail, and grows in scattered patches throughout the surrounding grasses. Intellectually I understand that poison ivy is native to this place, that it has a right to be here every bit as much as does the towering oak and the diminutive wild violet. Still, poison ivy was the annual scourge of my youth, and it wouldn't hurt my feelings very much if all of the poison ivy in all the world were to vanish suddenly. I do, however, find myself thinking about the so called "butterfly effect" that such a sudden disappearance might have. What, as yet unknown, purpose might this despised plant serve? Then again, must it serve a purpose or does it have an intrinsic right to life; a right free of any requirement that it serve some greater human need? I also recognize that in the ignorance of my youth I was to blame for much the misery I so often endured from contact with this plant. Reluctant as I am to admit it, only when I was in my late twenties, after years of intense itching and a particularly bad experience, did I finally decide I should learn what poison ivy looked like so that I could avoid it, since it didn't seem likely that it was going to avoid me.

The old Ferguson Road that bisects Ferguson Meadow is fringed with trees, a broken wall of green that divides the two sides of the field. The bridle trail approaches the eastern meadow through a narrow break in these trees. When observed from the west the eastern meadow first reveals itself as scattered patches of hazy sunlit vegetation, mosaic-like dapples of green, yellow, and tawny-brown, visible through the darker foliage that separates it from its wilder twin. Passing beneath trees that form an inviting gateway to the eastern meadow one is immediately presented with a panoramic view that is nothing less than stunning. This field, while never more than a couple of hundred yards wide, extends for perhaps a third of a mile to the east. As I wrote earlier, the eastern meadow has been maintained in a more open state, the trees and shrubs at its edges kept at bay. No creeping forest succession is in evidence here. Here tall grasses grow in an untidy uniformity that gives one the impression of a lawn in serious need of mowing.

The expansive view down the meadow is interrupted only at scattered points by small clumps of aging apple trees, their rough trunks encircled by uncut necklaces of high grass, daisies, and purple-headed thistle, their brittle branches hanging in senescent resignation. These trees appear to be the scattered and dying remnant of an early orchard. In *Pleasant Valley* Bromfield makes note of a ruined orchard near the meadow, evidence that these withered and weather-worn trees are from a much earlier day than Malabar Farm. A few additional mature apple trees grow within the woods along the northern fringes of the eastern meadow. These trees appear to be healthier than their meadow bound brothers. Perhaps they are younger, or perhaps they have been somewhat more sheltered from the stresses of a hundred icy winters and a hundred scorching summers. The dispirited trees of the meadow endure as little more than forlorn and lichen encrusted survivors of a lost orchard, overwhelmed now by both time and the elements. Bleak and nearly barren, they cleave only marginally to life, supporting little more than a thin scattering of listless leaves on the gnarled fingers of moribund branches.

Turning north onto the Ferguson Road I followed its shaded and deeply sunken route downhill, returning to the Butternut trailhead and Jim Pugh's cabin, and leaving behind the high and distant meadow, that place of solitude where Louis

Bromfield would go to regain a sense of balance in his often hectic life.

*There is something fey about the Ferguson place... You turn
to it when fear and depression assail you, with the instinct for
returning to the womb which Freud believed was strong in all of
us. In the lofty wilderness and solitude of the Ferguson Place one
goes back to the beginning of time.*

– Louis Bromfield
*Pleasant Valley* (1945)

# Chapter 6

# A Tale of Murder, A Very Rich Friend, and A Raucous Woodpecker

In the summer of 1896 an event, or rather a sequence of events, occurred in Pleasant Valley that to this day remain a large part of the folklore of the region. In October of that year, in a trial that drew observers from several surrounding counties, a young woman by the name of Celia Rose was found not guilty of the murder of her father. She was also declared criminally insane and committed to a State hospital, where she remained for the remainder of her life.

Though declared not guilty "by reason of insanity" Celia did indeed murder her father, as well as her mother and a brother. Her story has inspired a book that is illustrated with historic photographs and that includes many of the newspaper accounts of the events surrounding the deaths of the three Rose family members. Celia Rose's lethal deeds have also been dramatized in an award winning play written by Mark Jordan and produced by The Malabar Farm Foundation. The play, *Ceely*, is performed periodically in the Big Barn at Malabar Farm. This is a fitting

The Ceely Rose House, Malabar Farm State Park.

165

venue. The Rose family home, where the killings occurred, sits along Switzer Creek, less than a quarter of a mile from the barn. The infamous Ceely Rose House was part of the property included in the second farm that Louis Bromfield purchased in 1939.

The story of Celia Rose is a tale of unrequited love and murder, a story that is both sordid and sad. The Rose family came to Pleasant Valley from Pike County in southern Ohio in 1880. In that year David Rose purchased and began operating an old grist mill on Switzer Creek near his new home. Although the Rose family was thought of as somewhat odd, by 1896 they had become accepted as part of the valley community. David, at sixty-seven years of age, struggled to keep the mill going but was only

The old Charles Schrack mill, operated by David Rose in the late 19th century.
photograph courtesy Malabar Farm State Park

modestly successful at it. His wife Rebecca, two years younger, supplemented the family income by weaving rugs on a large loom in the parlor of their home. A son, Walter, aged forty, worked on and off as a farm hand in the valley. The only known photograph of Walter Rose gives one the impression of a drawn and gaunt man of somewhat limited intelligence, staring blankly to the side of the camera lens. Celia, twenty-three in 1896, has been described as tall and slightly overweight, with a moon face. She was also known to be quite frivolous and lazy. Celia was indulged by her parents and had few friends. A photograph of Celia was taken as she sat in jail awaiting her trial for murder. This photograph presents a curious image of the young woman. Her head is slightly cocked to one side, with the hint of a smile on her lips. She sits seemingly contented, aware of her situation, but not

Ceely Rose, awaiting trial, late summer 1896

photograph courtesy Malabar Farm State Park

particularly concerned about it. Thought by most to be somewhat odd and dimwitted, Celia was often called Silly Ceely Rose, sometimes even to her face. In was in the spring of 1896 that Celia first took special notice of a young man named Guy Berry who lived on the farm that adjoined the Rose property. Guy was five years younger than Celia and was considered a good looking and well-mannered young man. Celia began to strike up conversations with Guy at every opportunity. He responded politely with casual chit-chat, but that was the extent of his interest in Celia. Such was not the case with her. Mistaking his politeness for more than it was Celia's interest in Guy soon turned to infatuation, from infatuation it quickly devolved into obsession. She even went so far as to start telling people that Guy had proposed to her and that they were soon to be wed. Needless to say this unwanted attention soon began to cause Guy Berry considerable difficulty and embarrassment.

Finally, her parents stepped in and told Celia that she was making a fool of herself and was exposing the family to ridicule. She was to leave Guy Berry alone and was never again to speak of marriage, it wasn't going to happen. Celia took exception to her family's interference and soon devised a plan to remove this obstacle in her pursuit of true love. As a mill operator David Rose had a problem with rodents and kept on hand a good supply of a product called Rough-On-Rats. The main ingredient of this rat poison was arsenic. On the morning of June 24, 1896 Celia rose early, well before the rest of her family. In a burst of domestic energy uncharacteristic of her, she prepared a breakfast that included cottage cheese fresh from the spring house. After assuring herself that the others were still sleeping Celia retrieved the Rough-On-Rats from the mill and proceeded to dump several large spoons full of the pale green rat poison into the cottage cheese, then stirred it thoroughly until the powder had disappeared into the white curds. With that accomplished she hid the remainder of the poison behind the house and called her parents and brother down for breakfast.

That morning David Rose and his son Walter ate a hearty country breakfast, including two helpings of cottage cheese. Rebecca, complaining of a mild headache, ate sparingly. Celia only picked at her food and didn't touch the cottage cheese. With breakfast finished David left the house to begin his work in the mill. Walter headed up the Ferguson Road (see chapter 3) to gather berries he had been told were ripening. Rebecca and Celia cleared away the breakfast dishes. Rebecca then sat down at her loom. A short time later she began to complain of pains in her stomach and then began vomiting. Celia was sent to the mill to get her father. David found his wife writhing in pain on the kitchen floor and with Celia's help got her to bed. He then left for Newville to get the doctor. By the time he reached the doctor's home David himself was in appreciable pain. With considerable difficulty the doctor managed to get David home and to bed. Walter was found a short time later, lying semi-conscious and doubled up in pain in a ditch along the Ferguson Road. Apparently he had stumbled onto the road shortly after the doctor and David had passed.

Nothing that the doctor did could ease the suffering of David, Rebecca, and Walter. Celia complained of stomach pains but seemed not to be seriously ill. The doctor began to suspect some kind of poisoning. On June 30th, following six days of agony, David Rose died. Four days later, on Independence Day, Walter passed away. Rebecca, however, seemed to be recovering. With the two deaths, and the doctor's hunch of poisoning, the Richland County Prosecutor Augustus Douglas sent the county coroner to investigate. An autopsy of David's stomach verified that he had been poisoned with arsenic. Suspicion turned to Celia, but there was no evidence to back up the prosecutor's growing belief that somehow she was responsible for the deaths. By mid-July Rebecca had recovered to the point where she was able to move about the house and was again eating. The doctor even pronounced her recovered, but also told her that she should be careful with what she ate. Celia overheard this conversation and was not pleased. On July 19th she prepared a meal for her mother, and once again laced the food with the Rough-On-Rats. In her weakened condition Rebecca died that same day.

Following this third death Prosecutor Douglas found himself being pressured to solve what everyone now believed was a triple murder. Eventually he was able to recruit Tracy Davis, a twenty-year-old former schoolmate and sometime friend of

Celia's, to help him with a plan to trick Celia into confessing. Tracy had recently returned to the area and, as part of the plan she renewed her acquaintance with Celia. After building on their friendship for several weeks Tracy finally confided to Celia that she had a problem. She was in love with a young man and wanted to marry him, but her family and his family were feuding and her father refused to allow her to see him. She had tried everything she could think of, but had failed to change her father's mind. Could Celia think of anything she could say or do? After a long pause Celia told her new friend, "I think I can help you. I had a problem just like that. This is what I did." With that Celia began to relate in great detail how she had ended her parent's interference with her love life. Even now she was only waiting for things to calm down so that she and Guy could be wed. Unknown to Celia, Prosecutor Douglas and the county sheriff were hiding nearby and heard the confession. She was immediately arrested for murder.

Celia's trial at the Richland County Courthouse in October was attended by people from all over the county and from several counties bordering on Richland. Spectators spilled out of the courthouse and onto the surrounding sidewalks and streets. On October 20th Celia was found not guilty of murder but was declared insane. She was committed to a Women's Asylum in Toledo, and was later transferred to the State Hospital in Lima, Ohio. Celia Rose died there in 1934 at the age of sixty-one. Some people claim that on warm summer evenings when the cool mists of night have begun to obscure the fields of Pleasant Valley, and when the barred owls in the nearby woods begin to call to one another, the nebulous ghost of Ceely Rose can be seen at her bedroom window, peering longingly across Switzer Creek in the slowly fading light, searching for Guy, her long lost love.[21]

Today the Ceely Rose house sits empty, its leaf covered front porch facing Bromfield Road. Only a few yards separate the house from the beginning of Malabar Farm's Doris Duke Nature

Trail. This trail, a one mile loop through heavily wooded land, offers the most geologically interesting hike in the Park. It begins at the base of the hill where the old Ferguson/Newville Road, the road that once connected Pleasant Valley with the town of Newville, ends at Bromfield Road (see Chapter 3). The Ferguson Road is the road that Walter Rose took when he went berry picking, and the road that David Rose took on his way to fetch the doctor for his wife. It now takes visitors to the Malabar Farm Sugar Shack and Pugh Cabin. For today's automobile traffic the road ends at a small parking lot for the cabin and sugar shack, about a third of a mile up the hill and far short of Newville.

The trail was named in honor of Doris Duke (Duke University and The Duke Foundation). Her father, James Buchanan Duke, owner of the American Tobacco Company, dominated the tobacco industry during the first quarter of the 20th century. He managed his money well. Although no one knows exactly what he was worth, at the time of his death in 1925 his fortune was estimated to be between $60 and $100 million. In his will James Duke stipulated that $17 million was to be used to establish the Duke Endowment, aka The Duke Foundation. The remainder of his fortune was left to his wife and to his daughter Doris, who was only twelve when her father died. Through a series of bequests that she was to receive at ages twenty-one, twenty-five, and thirty, Doris Duke was referred to as "the world's richest woman." Shortly before his death Duke told his twelve-year-old daughter never to trust any man, as they would only be after her money. Doris Duke did have two marriages that ended badly, and she was involved in a long series of romantic relationships that were said to have included the likes of Errol Flynn, Duke Kahanamoku, General George Patton, and Louis Bromfield.

Duke first became personally acquainted with Louis Bromfield through his writing about agriculture and horticulture. At some point, probably in the early 1950s, she contacted him, asking for help in saving diseased elm trees on her estates. He replied, but had scant help to offer. Little could be done, because no effective treatment for Dutch Elm Disease existed. Perhaps she could cut down and burn the trees that were already showing signs of disease, then the others might live a little longer.

Through this initial contact a friendship developed between Duke and Bromfield. She visited Malabar Farm at least once, and for a time Bromfield stayed at her New Jersey estate while he was being treated for the bone cancer that would kill him only a short time later.

When Louis Bromfield died, he died in debt. Income from his novels had declined and some of his earlier works had actually gone out of print. Farm prices had bottomed out and the farm was losing money. He also had high medical bills from a year and a half of treatment for bone cancer and medical complications that had developed during treatment for that disease. Near his death he did something that must have caused him considerable anguish. To pay off his medical bills he sold the logging rights to the hillsides south of his Big House. He did stipulate that nothing under fourteen inches was to be cut. Louis Bromfield died believing the best of Malabar Farm's trees would fall. Shortly after his death Doris Duke was made aware of this timber sale and stepped in, purchasing the timber rights and returning them to his estate. Malabar Farm's beautiful forested hillsides are today blanketed in lush growth. Some of these trees are now over two-hundred years old and still growing, thanks to the generosity of Doris Duke. The trail that honors her gift loops through the best of the woods she saved.[22]

With its historical context firmly established in my mind it was time to explore the Doris Duke Woods itself. I chose a sunny, mid-October day for this, the last of the hikes to be included in this volume. The Doris Duke Trail is the most conveniently located trail at Malabar Farm, although all of them are easy to find. As I mentioned earlier, this trail begins across from the

Ceely Rose House, only a quarter of a mile from Louis Bromfield's Big House.

The morning sky was a bright blue, with tall trees providing a brilliant orange and yellow canopy over the beginning of my walk. The trailhead itself was bracketed by clusters of pale purple asters, past their prime, but still a pleasing contrast to the muddy browns of the shallow, pebble filled ditch that I stepped across to begin my hike. A few hundred feet into the woods the trail comes to a Y. This marks either the beginning or the end of the loop, depending on which way you choose to walk. I have hiked this trail many times over the years and I have usually turned to the right. Today would be no exception. Having turned right I followed the path as it parallels Bromfield Road for several hundred yards before it curves gradually to the south and away from the sounds of vehicle traffic, infrequent though they usually are. I take this direction because it is the shortest route to the most geologically interesting part of the trail. I almost never complete the loop, leaving it on the back side, where I hike off trail to a more remote, a more primeval portion of Malabar's woods, a place few people visit, a quiet place conducive to reflection and contemplation.

Not long after the proverbial fork in the trail I came upon an old and familiar friend, an entity I like to think of as the guardian of this particular forest. I am talking about an ancient and massive white oak. At the level of my shoulder it measures some four feet in diameter. Along its straight and thickly textured

There are still a few giants in the woods of Malabar Farm.

trunk are the scars of numerous broken branches and the swellings of several large burls. Rising perhaps to a height of fifty feet, its top is a weathered and splintered stub, evidence that it once reached considerably further skyward. Two-thirds of the way up the trunk two thick and gnarled branches extend outward like unsteady though still powerful and imposing arms. One arm is slightly higher than the other, both are nearly devoid of any smaller branches. Angling upward from one of these arms is the struggling growth of a singular living branch. This day it was adorned with a small vestige of russet colored leaves, these providing the only visible evidence that this forest giant still has life in it.

The trail beyond the ancient oak begins to rise gradually, still roughly parallel to, but climbing above Bromfield Road. Here the trail passes through a stand of a dozen or more eastern hemlocks. Only a few of these trees grow at Malabar Farm, so far removed from their natural habitat far to the north. About five or six miles from Malabar Farm, in a deep defile of the Mohican River in Mohican State Park, there are many more of these hemlocks. They thrive there, having found a suitable environment among the shaded rocks of a deep and steep-sided gorge, cut ages ago by the Mohican River. These eastern hemlocks, as well as the few that grow at Malabar, are descendants of hemlocks that thrived in this area fifteen to twenty thousand years ago, during the last ice age. How they came to be seeded on this hillside of Malabar Farm I do not know, but their evergreen presence offers a pleasing compliment to the October forest, its canopy and its floor ablaze with russet and scarlet reds, golden yellows, and pumpkin oranges, a warm artist's palate graciously shared by the maples, beech, and oaks that dominate this woodland.

Scattered throughout the Doris Duke woods are a number of old trees, senior citizens of this hillside, standing out by their size from the younger and smaller trees that surround them. On the desk in the study in Louis Bromfield's Big House there is a wintertime aerial photograph of this hillside, most likely taken in the late 1930s. It reveals that this slope was, in those days, only a sparsely wooded landscape, adorned with widely separated trees. The land between the trees is peppered with the black dots of numerous tree stumps. There is little evidence of any new growth taking place. One of Louis Bromfield's first acts upon purchasing this land was to rid his newly acquired woodlands of the grazing livestock that had been allowed to roam freely among the trees. Thus protected, this land began to heal and a forest to regenerate. Thanks to Louis Bromfield, and later to Doris Duke, we now have this wonderful maturing forest to enjoy.

Though oaks and maples prevail in these woods they share the landscape with a considerable number of beech trees, their smooth gray bark producing a striking contrast to the deep browns of the oaks and maples. Several of the beeches are of considerable size. Unfortunately more than one of these giants bear the scars of far too many past indiscretions by persons carrying pocket knives.

One of these beeches is of particular note. About eight feet above the ground this tree's thick trunk splits into two twin trunks. Below this split the tree is at least three feet in diameter. This beech and its aged neighbors are most likely among those trees photographed by that unknown pilot some seventy-five years ago. A scattering of black cherry trees also flourish here, their bark looking like burnt potato chips, their black trunks and branches standing out like silhouettes against the surrounding fall colors.

When I walk in these woods I usually do so rather slowly, being in no hurry to leave, taking ambles rather than hikes. From experience I have found that there is just too much to enjoy, too many things to experience that are overlooked when one is in a hurry. The slender shaft of sunlight that angles downward to illuminate a miniature forest of ground cedar, a satiny red beetle wandering the hills and valleys of last year's leaf fall, the ghostly white Indian Pipe timidly poking its head through decomposing forest litter, the rhythmic tapping of a near but unseen woodpecker, and the soft rustling of windblown leaves overhead, all pass unseen and unheard by those conditioned to think only in terms of hours expended and miles traveled. Overlooked is the wondrous expression of life revealed in the eye of a tiny tree frog. Lost is the realization that you may be the first and only human being that the little frog will ever see.

I almost always observe something new in the woods, and this walk was no exception. While scanning the forest floor several yards to the side of the trail I discovered the leaves of two trees that do not grow on this part of Malabar Farm, leaves that had, however, managed to find their way here. Laying atop the thick duff of oak, maple, and beech leaves was a single olive colored leaf from a sycamore. No more than a yard away from the sycamore leaf lay the yellowing leaf of a tulip poplar. I could find no other leaves of their kind nearby. While both of these trees are found at Malabar, I could see no parent to these leaves in the surrounding forest. Sycamore trees thrive near waterways and in wet areas. The closest water nearby is Switzer Creek, perhaps a quarter mile away. The same mystery surrounded the tulip poplar. Poplars are not especially common at Malabar and they are found in the Doris Duke woods in only one small and isolated spot not too far in from the trailhead. The tortuous route, presumably wind-borne, by which these singular leaves managed to find their way onto this oak, maple, and beech leaf blanketed forest floor can only be imagined.

Delightful woodland landscape aside, the thing that makes the Doris Duke Trail truly special is a pockmarked and much eroded sandstone cliff, several hundred yards in length. This cliff is the exposed face of the bedrock that the forest and the trail rest upon. Beginning about a quarter of a mile into the trail and roughly paralleling Bromfield Road, the cliff defines much of the northern side of the loop. The trail traces the upper edge of this ragged formation, the rocky outcropping falling precipitously away from it. This is one of my favorite places to explore. On this mild October day it also became a place of contemplation, a place to imagine the distant past, back to the time when these geological formations were first formed.

First, however, my attention was drawn toward the irregular border of the cliff, its hard surface softened by ferns and mosses. Approaching it I discovered that the cliff's edge was itself obscured beneath a low jumble of stones and small boulders, hundreds of rocks that I had never noticed before. They ranged in size from chicken's eggs to melons. It was no act of nature that had left these stones in heaps at this particular spot. A flat shelf of land runs back from the cliff's edge. A century or more ago this level ground must have been a farmer's field. When that unknown farmer first cleared this land he had collected these stones, piling them here, and throwing many more over the cliff's edge. Over the years many of these stones, sheltered beneath the gracefully curving fronds of hay scented ferns, have acquired a velvety patina of spongy green moss. Within the forest behind the stone

177

pile and the cliff's edge are several large beech trees. However, most of the trees here are fairly even in size, measuring from fifteen to eighteen inches in diameter, further evidence of this having been a field long ago. The presence of several rotting, though still quite large stumps does, however, suggest that other giants once lived here.

The trail follows the flat terrain along cliff's edge for several hundred yards before it turns away to begin a gradual uphill curve that will, should one choose to remain on the beaten path, eventually return the hiker to the trailhead and the Ceely Rose House. There was more to do today, however, than to quickly return to the day's beginning. The face of the cliff, varying from a dozen to more than twenty-five feet in height, is the imposing southeastern wall of the deep ravine that Bromfield Road travels as it climbs up and out of Pleasant Valley. At several places in this wall the sandstone has crumbled away over the ages. Blanketed with countless years of accumulated sandstone rubble and organic debris, these broad crevices had become natural ramps, pathways offering a precarious descent to the base of the cliff. By slowly and cautiously following one of these declines, I safely reached the bottom, knees aching but intact. I'm sure a younger person would have descended much more rapidly, but with age comes not only wisdom, but creaky knees and a much more guarded approach to taking chances.

Having reached the base of the cliff my thoughts were overwhelmed by a sense of primal timelessness. Ferns, prehistoric in their origin, grasped at my pant legs and tangled in my shoestrings. As I stepped carefully across the broken, rock strewn ground at the base of the coarsely textured sandstone I dragged my hand slowly along its surface, finger tips touching ancient seashore sands that, Medusa-like, had been turned to stone. These black-hand sandstone cliffs were born during the Early Mississippi Period some 350 million years ago, when this area was covered by a shallow inland sea. Over the span of millions of years, sand from distant mountains, carried on the currents of hundreds of rivers and streams, accumulated on the sea bed in great fan shaped deltas where sea and river met. This sand, slowly settling layer upon layer, had mixed with binding materials like iron oxide, the substance that gives some of these rocks their reddish appearance. Eventually the sand became the sedimentary sandstone rock layers that I could see and touch today.

Sea currents were not always consistent in these inland waters. Occasionally, the currents would change direction, depositing sand at an angle to that previously laid down. Geologists refer to this process as cross-bedding. The material that bonded these cross-bed layers was generally weaker. When sea currents returned to their normal patterns, sand would be deposited as it had been before and the sand particles would once again be bound together more tightly. Water that had carried the sand that settled into hard sedimentary layers would later be responsible for eroding the very rock that it had helped create.

Stepping back in time 350 million years..

The weaker, cross-bed layers were worn away more rapidly, forming the recesses and overhanging ledges that are visible

179

today. Water and weather also eroded softer stones that were embedded within sandstone. This process created the curious fist-sized honeycomb features that give added character and dimension to the sandstone formations of today.

Facing this ancient and craggy wall I turned my attention upward, eyes wandering across its coarse and multi-layered surface to where the rock ended in an uneven and fern fringed crown. Beyond the crown stood a vertical screen of tall trees. From my perspective far below them the trunks of the trees rose dramatically, their silhouetted forms narrowing to vanishing points in a high canopy of brightly colored October leaves. A glowing counterpane of oranges, yellows, and the jay blue of a clear fall sky hung suspended between earth and the heavens, the colors fractured into countless tiny fragments by a fine tracery of small black branches. Here was Mother Nature's very own cathedral, illuminated as dramatically as any medieval cathedral.

Earlier, while standing atop the cliff, I had remained a part of the world of men, a world of farmers who had cut trees, cleared fields, and piled stones up in great mounds, a world of men who had divided the land with fences, a world of men who created parks and then blazed trails through them. Nonetheless, in the process of descending to the bottom of this ancient world of ferns and frozen sand I had crossed an invisible line. I had stepped back in time, back across hundreds of millions of years of earth's history, back to a time long before the dinosaurs, back to a place old almost beyond comprehension. How does one, who counts his own existence in decades, relate to a world that is measured in eons?

An antediluvian environment of weathered brown rock, thigh high arcing ferns, lichens, deep green mosses, and spongy deadwood insinuated itself into my existential musings. For a few brief moments time was suspended and my imagination freed. I found myself wafting back across eons, back to the late Devonian and the Mississippian Periods, ages when fish ruled. In my mind's eye I seemed to be floating above it all. Below me was a vast sea that stretched southward to blend almost seamlessly with a distant horizon. To the north and east I could see an ancient seashore, its sandy beach washed with the parallel patterns of an endless tide. I could see the skittering trails of primitive invertebrates etched in the moist sand. I could see broad, shallow rivers hurrying to the sea through wide channels cut into a green landscape covered with the beginnings of great fern forests. Coming back to earth I leaned forward to draw a hand across the rough stone, momentarily awed by my own imaginings.

In hindsight I find it interesting that such strong and primeval emotions could so easily have been evoked, by turning my back to the sandstone cliff I could see Bromfield Road through the trees. It lay no more than two hundred yards away, across a deep ravine cut by a small, rock strewn creek. Rising abruptly from the road's far side was a second craggy sandstone wall, the slightly smaller and somewhat less exposed twin to the cliff that I stood below. The glint of a blue sky, reflected in silvery pools of water laying in the shadowed depths of the ravine, gave evidence of the patient forces that had cut into and exposed these sandstone foundations. This ravine had not only separated me physically from the highway, but had also separated me psychologically. The charcoal gray ribbon of asphalt, so close at hand, had disturbed neither my solitude nor my thoughts. I do suspect that a passing automobile would have broken the magical spell. Fortunately none did so this day. The air had remained still, contemplation reigned and imagination flowed as freely as the little stream below me. I had been lifted out of time, if only for a few moments.

One can remain tethered to such daydreaming for only so long and soon it was time to leave. I followed the base of the cliff along a rugged landscape of sharp rocks, drooping Christmas ferns, rotting logs, and moss covered boulders, to where another break in the sandstone wall offered a relatively easy scramble upward to the cliff's top. Apparently a chipmunk had been reflecting on his own place in the great scheme of things. I had barely gained the cliff's upper edge when the little fellow began a rebuking chatter strongly suggesting that I was only a guest in his world, and evidently not a very welcome one at that. Jumping from rock to log and back to rock again, at no time more than a dozen feet in front of me, he would pause to bark his displeasure, then was off again. After a minute or so of this frenetic activity, apparently satisfied that he had taken me to task, the chipmunk disappeared into a tiny cavern formed where a tree had fallen against a small pile of stones at the edge of the cliff. I turned to find the trail and continue my walk through Doris Duke's Woods. Except for the cawing of distant crows and the buzzing of unseen insects, this chipmunk's voice had been the only animal sound I had encountered so far on this most quiet of my Thousand Acre walks.

I regained the trail where it turns away from the cliff. Here the ground rises gradually to the south and passes alongside a collection of quite mysterious shallow pits. Leaf covered and concealed beneath an accumulation of fallen branches and small tree trunks, it takes a little searching to find them, and I expect

Peering into the largest of the mysterious circular
depressions on the Doris Duke Trail.

that most passers-by never notice them. I myself had missed them on my first few walks through these woods. The largest of them, lying only a few hundred feet back from the sandstone cliff, measures about twelve feet in diameter. Most of the other depressions range from about six to eight feet across. They appear to be about one to two feet deep, though their original depth is hard to determine, as they are now filled with forest debris that has most likely been accumulating for decades, if not centuries.

What makes these depressions so strange is that they are all nearly perfectly formed circles. These are not the irregular hollows formed when giant trees crash to the ground, uplifting massive amounts of root, rock and soil as they fall. No hummocks of dirt and rock border these pits. There is no evidence of massive trunks that have slowly decomposed and disappeared back into the earth, leaving in their wake a telltale line of moss as evidence of their former existence. No rocks of any size can be seen within the concave bottoms of the pits, though all are cluttered with fallen branches and twigs, and a few of the pits have small saplings sprouting within them. The level rims of these depressions appear disturbed only by the growth of the surrounding forest as it has pushed up against them in the years since their creation.

Wandering slowly through the area I counted at least twenty-one of these curious pits within a rectangle that measures roughly fifty by one-hundred-fifty yards. In some places these depressions are clustered together in twos or threes, separated by only a few feet, while others are separated by dozens of yards. The exactness of these circles suggests that they were man-made, but I can only guess at what the depressions are, who created them, why, and when. The Lenape Indians occupied this area in the eighteenth and early nineteenth centuries. Might these pits have been the remnants of a village, the shallow circles all that now remain of their lodges? As Indian villages were usually located near water I am hesitant to offer this possibility too vigorously, but no better explanation immediately comes to mind. They are a mystery and they will most likely remain so until some future excavation reveals their secrets.

Leaving the mystery of the depressions behind, I continued my walk, following the trail gradually uphill as the path curved to the east to complete the loop. On my right, visible through the trees near the top of the hill, was a sunlit clearing carved out of the surrounding woods. This is the little used Malabar Farm picnic area, and this marked the point where I planned to leave the trail. Those few people who do enjoy the picnic grounds usually reach it by a more conventional route, the paved road that spurs off of Bromfield Road just beyond the ravine and the sandstone cliffs. Approaching it from my woodland direction I couldn't follow such a direct route, finding it necessary to navigate around several thorny obstacles. The forest's sunlit understory near the grassy edge of the picnic area is choked with thick snarls of multi-flora rose bushes, their countless arching stems spreading out helter-skelter, each one armed with hundreds of jabbing barbs. It took some weaving and dodging to pass through this thorny welter. It also required a willingness to endure repeated snags to my pant legs and shoelaces and not a few jabs to bare arms before I could step into the sun filled clearing, with its collection of weathered wooden tables, and its scattering of pole mounted blue bird boxes. This is actually the best place I have found in the Park to see blue birds. Though none appeared today I have often seen them in this area, blue dots streaking across the sky from box to forest and back to box again in search of their bug lunch. It does require some patience and stillness to photograph these elusive birds, but they will usually appear once they had become comfortable with a quiet human presence.[23]

On this particular October day the numerous sugar maples that shade the picnic tables where glowing in the bright sunlight, aflame with extravagant blends of orange, yellow, and hints of scarlet. Having seated myself at a picnic table for a few moments,

I turned my face skyward. Gazing into the thick cover of leaves that hung overhead was like looking at the best of the stained glass windows of any medieval cathedral. Could the otherworldly wonder of Chartres, Notre Dame, or Reims offer anything more inspiring than an American hardwood forest in the autumn?

Beyond the blacktop lane and parking area that marks the southern boundary of the picnic ground there is a wooden pit-toilet that backs up to a deep forest. With my brief stay in the sun at an end I stepped into that dark woods, entering into what is one of my favorite locations within Malabar Farm's thousand acres. The picnic ground sits upon a level ridge, but on entering the woods on the ridge's south side the land immediately begins to fall away in a gentle decline through a landscape of mature trees and small sandstone outcroppings. This part of Malabar's forest remains as I imagine it might have looked when the Lenape Indians hunted here, and when the earliest white pioneers lost their way in what must have seemed to them an endless forest. Tall trees, oaks, maples, beech, and a scattering of black cherry and hickory, rise loftily overhead, all of them adorned with thick crowns of interwoven branches and leaves. The shade from this thick leafy covering keeps the forest floor relatively free of underbrush. Multi-flora has made only sporadic inroads here. Most of what does grow beneath these giants is their own off-spring, small saplings patiently awaiting their time in the sun. When one of their elders, succumbing to age, weather, or disease, finally does crash to the forest floor a hole will be opened to the sky. Sunlight, the proverbial "light in the forest," will stream in. Young trees, exposed for the first time to the full energy of this direct sunlight, will accelerate their climb toward the sky. Gradually the hole will disappear, repeating a cycle of growth, death and decay that is as old as there are trees in this forest.

A new bridle trail has recently been cut into the hillside a few hundred feet below the picnic area. This new path does, unfortunately, take away a little of the primal feel of these woods.

185

Still, by moving a hundred yards or so beyond the trail my imagination was once again transported back to an earlier day and another world, a world without clocks and without schedules. I found a friendly rock to rest on so that I could enjoy a more relaxed consideration of my surroundings. Inspired by a forest of towering trees, with tired feet settled upon a thick carpet of parchment leaves, and with a gentle breeze playing ancient tunes in the branches high overhead, my attention drifted to thoughts of time and transition. An image of time as an unending thread formed in my mind, certainly not an original idea. However, in this evocative setting the originality of the notion seemed immaterial. I could see the days and nights, the seasons and the years extending backward and forward endlessly, each moment of time in perpetual flux, impossible to hold, the present only a moving pinpoint separating past and future. Lifting my eyes skyward to gaze through the dark calligraphic lines of countless branches, through the shimmering canopy of red, gold and orange leaves, and beyond the leaves to patches of blue sky, I could imagine that I was seeing the same timeless vision that my grandfathers of a hundred generations past had seen.

Many years ago I took a wintertime evening's walk down the road that led to my grandfather's farm house. He had died a few months earlier and I was in a reflective mood. Pausing along the snow filled lane that led to his old barn, I had turned my eyes upward to the moon, shining bright and silver cold through the darkened branches of the numerous locust trees that bordered the lane. It came to me in a spontaneous rush of emotion that this was a sight that my grandfather, and his father, and the countless grandfathers that had preceded us, had themselves witnessed. This was the same crater filled moon, the same dark sky, the same sparkle of starlight. Death is a strange thing, although distanced from my grandfather by time and passing, I was still able to share this experience with him. Decades later there would come this brief moment, sitting upon a sandstone boulder on a wooded hillside on a sun filled fall day at Malabar

Farm, when those same emotions, feelings that had been generated long ago by a winter night and an icy moon, would surface again. I could experience the same wonder of nature's creation as had my great-great grandfathers, the same sights that had inspired awe, reverence, and perhaps not a little fear in the hearts and minds of countless generations of people who had preceded even them.

An impression of a personal "circle of life" began to form in my mind's eye. The thread of time that had no beginning and no end became the line that formed the circle, with myself, my ancestors and my descendants all finding our place upon it; past, present, and future, each of us being an essential piece of the loop. Does that mean that somewhere along that line my grandfather still lives? Who knows, as singer, and songwriter Iris DeMent voiced it, "let the mystery be" Thinking forward to some distant day I can imagine a descendant of mine sitting in these woods. He might rest upon this same gray rock, surrounded at that time by a new generation of trees. He might turn his face skyward and his mind might wonder back to the time when we, his ancestors, gazed skyward through our forest. Then his thoughts might embrace all of us, as mine did my ancestors on this day. Such were my thoughts, perhaps a little illogical, perhaps a little maudlin, inspired by the abundant sights, smells, textures, and colors of a mature hardwood forest in fall.

Rising from my musings I once again entered the more temporal world of the October forest. From where I had been sitting the hillside's topography slopes down in gently undulating steps. These rolling ups and downs give a pleasing variety to the forest floor, studded as it is with moss covered boulders. In mid-October the ferns, both the frilly hay-scented and evergreen Christmas, still stand tall in lush clusters, and barberry shrubs hang heavy with red fruit. Sulfur Shelf, (aka Chicken mushroom), continues to thrive for a few more days on dead trees, but the Chanterelles are past their prime. Not being schooled in the art of mushroom identification these two mushrooms and the brainy looking and highly prized morel are the only three wild mushrooms I dare to eat. Why risk eating something called "Destroying Angel?"

Continuing through the open woods in a generally south-east direction I soon came upon a wide area of low, table-like, sandstone outcroppings. One in particular rose a foot or two above the surrounding forest floor. It looked like a stony iceberg floating serenely on the forest floor, most of its volume hidden beneath the ground. The relatively flat surface of the rock was split into several smaller sections by deep fissures, creating great jig-saw like pieces. The gray and coarsely textured top of the stone was partially covered with a softening blanket of sea-green lichens and olive green mosses. Autumn leaves, scattered randomly across the gray-green surface, added further color to the rich natural patina of the outcropping. Exploring a little further I discovered that this sandstone outcropping was the exposed rear portion of the roof of the massive sandstone monolith that formed the Malabar Farm Cave that I described in an earlier chapter. By leaving the Doris Duke trail and turning south I had come out above and behind the cave. From here it was a simple matter to locate the Butternut Trail and follow it back to the Pugh Cabin, also highlighted earlier. This section of the Butternut Trail, the short section that linked the cabin to the cave, has for years been the most heavily used portion of any trail in the park. It is a wide path and quite easy to follow. Its surface is tightly compacted and smooth, disturbed only by the irregular lattice-work of hundreds of blackened and interlocking roots, worn smooth and polished to an almost satiny finish by the passage of countless shoes and boots.

I had this well-worn trail entirely to myself, and so tramped leisurely along its broad avenue in complete solitude. Contrary to what I had expected, it was here, in a place frequently disturbed by the happy voices of families and excited school children on field trips, that the forest finally came alive with its own movement and sound. Considering my hike nearly over I was surprised to hear the muffled snapping of twigs to the right of the trail. Nearly hidden among the trees, their tawny coats providing excellent camouflage, were two deer, both does. Apparently startled by my appearance, they hastened to put distance between themselves and me. Only the upturned flag of their white tails gave evidence of their rapid departure. Hunting isn't permitted in the Park so the deer here show relatively little fear of man. They do, however, always maintain a certain cautious distance from me when I have wandered into their domain. Today was no exception and the pair was soon gone, having blended seamlessly into the woodland background.

Only a few yards further on I was halted again, this time by the warning chatter of a quite incensed black squirrel. Unlike the deer, who had quietly and graciously relocated their personal space further away, this dark gentleman stood his ground, letting me know that I was an unwelcome interloper on his turf. His tiny feet were planted firmly on a fallen log, the arched plume of his tail quivering rapidly in a blur of black fur. Agitated, rapid-fire chirping left no doubt as to his irritation with my presence. After a few moments of this bellicose denunciation he deftly leaped to a nearby tree, quickly vanishing behind its far side. A moment later he poked his black head around to check on me, then scampered down to disappear into the woods. He briefly reappeared on a more distant log where he again repeated his indignant vocalizations. This final outburst continued for only few moments before he finally gave up the field and vanished into the cover of deeper woods.

Black squirrels are a melanistic sub-group of gray squirrels. They can exist wherever grays live. Although gray squirrels abound in Malabar's woods it has only been in the past year that I have started seeing a few black squirrels here. Perhaps they have been here all along and I just never noticed. If that is the case then I am disappointed with my observation skills, because these little black creatures with their contentious chattering are hard to miss. Years ago I observed a large population of black squirrels on the campus of Kent State University, but prior to this year of walking the trails at Malabar Farm I had seen but one other black squirrel, that being a solitary individual, observed while on a hike in a remote area of northwestern Pennsylvania's Allegheny National Forest.

As I approached the Pugh Cabin near the end of the Butternut Trail one final woodland surprise awaited me. The incensed black squirrel had apparently passed his torch of indignation to a large pileated woodpecker. I heard the bird's piercing staccato call before I actually saw his large black form swoop across my path to land on the side of a tree some twenty or thirty feet to my right. Clinging to the rough bark of a white oak, his coal black feathered back facing me, he slowly rotated his scarlet crested head in my direction. Our eyes met for a moment, then he quickly lifted off, settling once again on a tree further down the trail. His piercing squawks, I would be insincere if at this point I were to call them bird song, continued intermittently, as for the next several minutes he engaged in a series of brief sorties, skipping from one tree to another, crisscrossing the trail in front of me with each new flight. By these clipped aerial maneuvers he was able to maintain a guarded space between us as I slowly made my way down the trail. He seemed unwilling to abandon this patch of his woods without at least the appearance of protest. Finally the woodpecker drifted away and was quickly lost in the enveloping forest thicket. Apparently he had concluded that I posed no serious threat, and that further protestation was not worth the energy.

I have always considered it a privilege to spot a pileated woodpecker in the wild. These, the largest of the woodpeckers, favor the deep woods and their presence in Malabar's heavily forested southern hills is a welcome sight. I am not alone in my appreciation of this big black fellow with the bright scarlet head. This woodpecker has a special place in Hollywood film lore, a place that blends quite well with both Louis Bromfield's love of nature and the many Hollywood guests that he hosted at Malabar Farm.[24] A pileated woodpecker was the inspiration for Walter Lantz's beloved cartoon character Woody Woodpecker, though the circumstances of Woody's birth are something of a question. As the "official" story goes, it was 1940 and Walter Benjamin Lantz was an independent producer supplying cartoons to Universal Studios. That year Lantz's honeymoon with actress Grace Stafford was repeatedly interrupted by the loud and incessant hammering of a large pileated woodpecker as it pounded holes into their cottage roof. Lantz wanted to shoot the bothersome bird, both to end the vexing noise and to protect the roof from further damage. Grace suggested that instead of killing it he should study the bird and develop a cartoon based on it.

That is the movie studio's story, but it has some problems. Apparently Walter Lantz and Grace Stafford weren't married until after Woody's first film appearance, and Mel Blanc, who provided Woody's voice for his first three cartoons, had used Woody's signature staccato laugh in several earlier Warner Brothers cartoons. Though the details of his birth may be in doubt, his subsequent film success isn't. Woody Woodpecker made his screen debut late in 1940 in an Andy Panda cartoon. Although not the main character, Woody stole the show and secured his future in show business. Between 1940 and 1972 he starred in nearly 100 films. Between 1957 and 1966 Woody even had his own television show. In 1972 Woody Woodpecker retired, but he has occasionally come out of retirement to make special appearances, including a cameo appearance in the 1988 feature film *Who Framed Roger Rabbit.*

The final quarter-mile of the trail, enlivened as it had been by the spirited sights and sounds of the surrounding forest, presented a satisfying conclusion to my hike, the final walk at Malabar Farm to be included in this book about Malabar's green hills and valleys. I passed the Pugh Cabin and Malabar's Sugar Shack, then followed the tree lined and hard packed earth of William Ferguson's old road down to Bromfield Road and the Doris Duke trailhead, where my walk had started hours earlier. Across Bromfield Road I could see the ill-famed Ceely Rose House. Its white clapboard siding glowed with the warmth of the afternoon sun. The cheerful, welcoming luminosity of the sunlight falling across the house presented a sharp contrast to the dark tragedy that had occurred within its walls.

The Rose family's aging frame house and the grist mill that once stood behind it... Captain Pipe's cliff and the long lost Indian village of Helltown... the sandstone cave and the ancient and worn sandstone cliffs... the Olivet Cemetery... the Ferguson Road that once led to the town of Newville... Louis Bromfield's Malabar Farm itself, edged now by wooded hillsides that were saved through Doris Duke's generosity... all of these have been bound together in the tightly woven fabric of the rich story that has made these thousand acres and the surrounding countryside of Pleasant Valley of such special interest and value to me.

Perhaps someday our paths will cross, yours and mine, on one of Malabar Farm's delightful trails, until then may all your hikes be sunny and your feet dry.

*There is a rhythm in life, a certain beauty which operates by a variation of lights and shadows, happiness alternating with sorrow, content with discontent, distilling in this process of contrast a sense of satisfaction, of richness that can be captured and pinned down only by those who possess the gift of awareness.*

− Louis Bromfield

## Epilogue

# An End and a New Beginning

*He hears with gladdened heart the thunder*
*Peal, and loves the fallen dew;*
*He knows the earth above and under—*
*Sits and is content to view.*
— Robert Louis Stevenson

At the time of his death Louis Bromfield had a will that contained some vague language giving the trustees of his estate "uncontrolled discretion" to see that income from the operation his farm be used for its continuance. He left no specific instructions, however, pertaining to the long-range future of Malabar Farm. Under the trustees' absentee direction the farm struggled on, but it was seriously hampered by the lack of money and the fact that several farm implement companies, companies that had previously been anxious to lend equipment to Malabar Farm for the publicity, upon hearing of Louis Bromfield's death, rushed in and repossessed their equipment. This, and the reality that the guiding spirit of Louis Bromfield was gone, made the continued operation of the farm something of a sad affair. The farm hands who had worked with "The Boss" slowly began to drift away.

When he died Louis Bromfield was in debt. In 1956 he still had an income of about $40,000 annually from his writing, but that figure didn't approach his earlier earnings. He was supporting a farm, a home, and a manner of living that he could no longer afford. Some of his earliest books were going out of print, agricultural prices had declined steeply during the mid-1950s, and he had high medical bills from treatments for bone cancer and the complications resulting from it. Following his

194

death, Bromfield's estate lawyers kept Malabar operating for about a year. By 1957 the financial situation of the farm had, however, become untenable, and the trustees of his estate prepared for its dissolution. Advertisements and brochures were prepared offering the sale of Malabar Farm. It seemed that Louis Bromfield's dream, the capstone to his long and celebrated career, would dissolve into some stranger's real estate development.

Fortunately that did not happen. Thanks to the efforts of several Bromfield friends, and especially the dedicated leadership of good friend, Ralph Cobey, the farm was saved. In May of 1957 the trustees of the Louis Bromfield estate sold Malabar Farm to the Friends of the Land, a national conservation organization that Bromfield had been a prominent member of. A year later The Friends of the Land sold the property to Ralph Cobey and four other gentlemen. To purchase the farm Mr. Cobey personally provided a loan of $15,000, with an additional $40,000 coming from a dozen other individuals. This money was added to $127,535 secured in the form of several promissory notes from the Samuel Roberts Noble Foundation of Oklahoma. The notes held by the Noble Foundation were to be paid in full by November 1966. The Noble Foundation, while not involved in the operation of Malabar Farm, would hold the mortgage on the property.[25]

In December of 1958 the Louis Bromfield Malabar Farm Foundation was formed, with Ralph Cobey as its first president. The Foundation, guided by a board of three trustees, took over operation of the farm and it would continue as a working farm. There would also be an agricultural education program dedicated to promoting the agricultural practices of soil conservation, sustainability, and food nutrition, what Louis Bromfield called the "New Agriculture." These were practices that had earned Bromfield the unofficial title, "Father of Sustainable Agriculture." Both Malabar Farm and Louis Bromfield's beloved Big House would be open to the public for tours.

For reasons I have never fully understood Malabar Farm, even though under the non-profit status of the Foundation, was never able to make a success of the property. November, 1966 came and went with no loan payments on either principle or interest having been made to the Noble Foundation. By 1972 Malabar Farm was nearly a quarter of a million dollars in debt. Although the Noble Foundation was not pressing the Louis Bromfield Malabar Farm Foundation for its money, changes in Federal laws pertaining to non-profit organizations made it necessary for the Noble Foundation to do something about the long over-due debt. Years earlier the possibility of the State of Ohio acquiring Malabar Farm had been discussed, but the State's Department of Natural Resources had not been interested. When a new administration took office in Columbus the subject was raised again. This time, with the approval of Governor John Gilligan, the State entered discussions aimed at the possibility of Malabar Farm becoming State property.

In Louis Bromfield's first non-fiction farm book *Pleasant Valley,* published in 1945, he wrote of the possibility that some day "the hills, valleys and woods" of Malabar might be owned by the State. In that expression he implied that Malabar Farm should be open to the public for all to enjoy and learn from. In 1972 this possibility came true. Following a series of negotiations between all of the interested parties, the Noble Foundation, in exchange for receiving the deed to the property, released the mortgage that it held on Malabar Farm. The Noble Foundation then gave Malabar Farm to the State of Ohio for $1, doing so with the understanding that the farm was to be operated in a manner that would be in accordance with Louis Bromfield's conservation philosophy. Now owned by the State of Ohio and operated by the Ohio Department of Natural Resources, Malabar Farm became Malabar Farm State Park in 1976, on the 20th anniversary of Louis Bromfield's death.[26]

From the time that Louis Bromfield first began to buy

property in Pleasant Valley in January of 1939 through today, Malabar Farm has remained a working farm, and is perhaps the author's most enduring legacy.

*Our house is a big house, well built, to be used not only by ourselves but by friends and neighbors as well, and by generations after we are dead.*

—Louis Bromfield, *Pleasant Valley,* 1945

1. In creating Malabar Farm Louis Bromfield purchased three smaller farms and the "Jungle", totaling about 600 acres. He also leased nearly two hundred acres from Pleasant Hill Reservoir, part of the Muskingum Watershed Conservancy District. The State of Ohio acquired Malabar Farm in 1972. Over the next five years it added almost 400 additional acres of woodlands to Malabar's original 600.

2. Louis Bromfield's wife, sister, father, and mother preceded him in death and are also buried at Olivet Cemetery.

3. The Louis Bromfield Malabar Farm Foundation operated Malabar Farm until 1972 when the property was given to the State of Ohio. Malabar Farm became Malabar Farm State Park in 1976.

4. Only about 1% of our nation's virgin forest survives east of the Mississippi River. The largest expanse of this original forest survives in The Great Smokey Mountain National Park in Tennessee and North Carolina.

5. One avian call that I do recognize isn't that of a song bird. It is the plaintive call of the barred owl. Hearing its probing "Who, Who, Who Cooks For You?" while snug within my sleeping bag in a darkened tent, settled in the depths of a nighttime forest, never fails to stir my imagination or to sharpen my appreciation for all things natural and wild. Writing of the song of wood thrush, Henry Thoreau had the following to say in his journal entry for June 22, 1853; *"All that is ripest and fairest in the wilderness is preserved and transmitted to us in the strain of the wood thrush. This is the only bird whose note affects me like music... It is inspiring. It is a meditative draught to my soul.*

6. Although the house had burned down years before, the crumbling remains of the log cabin survived into the 1940s. Louis Bromfield included a photograph of it in the first edition of *Out of*

*the Earth.*

7. As late as the mid-1960s the Louis Bromfield Malabar Farm Foundation was touting the benefits of the multi-flora rose. In their newsletter they bemoaned the fact that many of these thorny "natural fences" had been killed during an especially severe winter.

8. Jim Pugh used many of these Newville stones to construct the chimney and landscaping walls of his 1938 log cabin on the forested hillside that would soon be surrounded by Louis Bromfield's Malabar Farm. Today the cabin is part of Malabar Farm State Park.

9. It would be only a few miles from Pinhook, beyond rolling hills to the southwest, that a hundred and twenty-five years later Louis Bromfield would establish Malabar Farm.

10. In 1846 the remaining eastern portion of Green Township became part of newly organized Ashland County.

11 .David and Elizabeth Schrack had three sons and eleven daughters (Three of the children died in infancy and two are believed to have remained in Pennsylvania.) Their house must have been a quite crowded and busy place.

12. Four more children would be born after the move to Richland County: Jane, born c.1824; William, born 1837, Ann, and Joseph.

13. There is a photograph of the remains of William Ferguson's log cabin in the first edition of Louis Bromfield's *Out of the Earth.*

14. Unfortunately a mistake was made on the familiar white veteran's memorial stone erected in the Olivet Cemetery to honor George Baughman. On that stone his birth date was erroneously

engraved as 1828.

15. So called because all parts of the plant are poisonous except the pea sized fruit. It was once believed that this plant was a primary ingredient in many a witch's bubbling caldron of potions.

16. I walked that boardwalk on the hike described here, but by then many of its planks had become rotted and dangerous. By the time I wrote these words the trail had been re-routed onto dry ground running alongside the wetland. The boardwalk did provide an opportunity to closely examine the skunk cabbage and the marshy earth, but its removal was better for both the land and hikers.

17. Louis Bromfield raised both beef and dairy cattle. If the many photographs taken at Malabar during his years on the farm are any indication, I believe he favored his dairy herd.

18. In geological vocabulary this natural feature is a crack in the rock, not a true cave, a cave being a passageway underground. I refer to it here and elsewhere as a cave simply for convenience and to honor local tradition.

19. This hillside was part of the Clem Herring property, the first farm that Louis Bromfield would buy in creating Malabar Farm.

20. Ferguson Meadow is divided into a large eastern side and a smaller western side by the old Ferguson/Newville Road. See Chapter Three.

21. Guy Berry left the area after Ceely had become the primary suspect in the Rose murders. He returned to Pleasant Valley only after she was safely locked away. Guy lived to be 82 years old. He died in 1961 and was buried in the Pleasant Valley Lutheran Cemetery, near the graves of David, Rachel, and Walter Rose.

22. There is some disagreement in the sources as to exactly how the Duke money was spent. There is no question, however, that Doris Duke did donate $30,000 to the Friends Of The Land, and that shortly afterward the timber rights were bought back and the trees saved.

23. I have recently been told that a 40' x 60' picnic shelter is to be constructed at the picnic area.

24. Humphrey Bogart and Lauren Bacall were married at Malabar Farm on May 21, 1945. Louis Bromfield, a good friend of Bogart, served as his best man. Additional Hollywood regulars at Malabar included James Cagney, Ann Frances, and Joan Fontaine.

25. Lloyd Noble, a friend of Louis Bromfield's, had made a fortune in Oklahoma oil. He created the Noble Foundation in 1945 to honor his father Samuel Noble. The Noble Foundation, remains active today, supporting the study and practice of soil conservation and sustainable agriculture.

26. See **www.malabarfarm.org** for what is happening at Malabar Farm today.

Manufactured by Amazon.ca
Bolton, ON

11114442R00111